TRANSFORMING summer programs

AT YOUR LIBRARY

OUTREACH *and* OUTCOMES *in* ACTION

NATALIE COLE
VIRGINIA A. WALTER

D1205850

ALA Editions

An imprint of the American Library Association
Chicago / 2018

ISBN: 978-0-8389-1628-5 (paper)

Library of Congress Cataloging in Publication Control Number: 2017052415

Cover design by Alejandra Diaz. Images © Adobe Stock. Book design and composition by Kimberly Thornton in the Museo Slab and Chaparral typefaces.

⊗ This paper meets the requirements of ANSI/NISO Z39.48–1992 (Permanence of Paper).

Printed in the United States of America

22 21 20 19 18   5 4 3 2 1

TRANSFORMING

summer
programs

AT YOUR LIBRARY

CONTENTS

FOREWORD

GREG LUCAS / *California State Librarian*

The only constant in this world is change. Libraries have been around for thousands of years, but they're far different institutions now than they were 100 years ago, 20 years ago, or even just 5 years ago. Part of that change lies in how libraries provide summer programming, as Natalie Cole and Virginia Walter discuss in the next 200 pages or so. And believe me, it's changing. The California State Library supports "Summer @ Your Library: Explore, Learn, Read, Connect." If the name of this program doesn't tell you things have changed, nothing will. Natalie and Virginia describe a lot of these changes, which help better engage community members and make learning more fun.

There is value in this book's examples for librarians in other states and for other state librarians. Pete Seeger tells a story about Woody Guthrie being asked what he thought about Bob Dylan. Guthrie laughed and said, "Dylan just steals from me. I steal from everybody." There is plenty of good stuff to steal from plenty of good people in the pages ahead.

One of my favorite changes in summer programming is offering free lunches for poor kids. Hunger doesn't go on vacation when public schools let out for three months, and an increasing number of libraries and librarians are helping address this most basic of needs. In California in 2014, 17 libraries began serving lunches. In just a few short years, there are now 160 California libraries doing this. Having visited several of these Lunch at the Library programs around the state, I've noticed a common thread—as folks finish lunch, they ask about signing up for other summer programming, particularly reading programs.

Reimagining summer library programming is just one of the ways that new generations of librarians are reconfiguring the relationships libraries have with their community. These librarians are more than happy to find whatever you're looking for, but that's just one part of their desire to change the world. One library user at a time, if necessary.

And since change is inevitable, isn't it better to help make it as positive as possible?

ACKNOWLEDGMENTS

The transformation of summer in California's libraries is happening because of the dedication of library staff across the state.

Thank you to all California library staff who have advised on and helped to develop the Summer @ Your Library outcome- and outreach-based framework, quality principles and indicators, and programming and outreach projects. The Summer @ Your Library resources—and this book—could not have been created without you.

Thank you to all California library staff who have hosted and taken part in trainings and meetings, provided feedback on program developments, shared their stories, successes, challenges, and lessons learned, and who have furthered the conversation around summer programming in California's public libraries.

Thank you to all California library staff who have served as iREAD California committee members and provided theme-based resources and training to help California libraries implement their summer programs each year. Thank you to our friends and colleagues at the Southern California Library Cooperative and Califa for their contributions to the Summer @ Your Library project. And thank you to our iREAD friends and colleagues in Illinois, who help us provide California's library staff with high-quality programming resources each year.

Thank you to Trish Garone, project manager extraordinaire, whose thoughtful and dedicated work makes the Summer @ Your Library project happen; Shana Sojoyner, for supporting the library staff who use the outcome- and outreach-based framework; Katie Brackenridge, for her contributions to the Summer Matters chapter of this book, and everyone working in support of the Summer Matters campaign; and Patrice Chamberlain, for cowriting the Lunch at the Library chapter of this book, for her partnership, her tireless efforts to provide California's children and teens with summer meals, and her passionate support for libraries.

Thank you to Cindy Mediavilla for her advice, guidance, and feedback on the manuscript, and to Jonathan Furner for his herculean effort with the references.

Thank you to the California Library Association for managing and championing the Summer @ Your Library project, and to the California State Library and the Institute of Museum and Library Services for their continued support of summer programming in California's public libraries. And thank you to Jamie Santoro for giving us the opportunity to share this California story.

On a personal note, Natalie Cole would like to thank Rita Cole and Robert Cole for their unwavering love and support, and Jonny, Zak, and Lucas for being the best family anyone could ask for. Virginia A. Walter would like to thank the UCLA students who have inspired her in class and gone on to brilliant careers in public libraries.

Case studies for this book were contributed by:

Lana Adlawan, Oakland Public Library
Allison Angell, Benicia Public Library
Ivonne Arreola, Whittier Public Library
Kim Brown, California State Library
Chris Curley, San Diego County Library
Jodi de la Pena, San Diego County Library
Lori Easterwood, fomerly of Sacramento Public Library
Melissa Elliott, Burbank Public Library
Christy Estrovitz, San Francisco Public Library
Amanda Foulk, Sacramento Public Library
Lisa Gonzalez, Santa Barbara Public Library
Christie Hamm, Sacramento Public Library
Katherine Jardine, San Francisco Public Library
Michelle Jeffers, San Francisco Public Library
Nina Lindsay, Oakland Public Library
Mary McCasland, Buena Park Library District

Carey McKinnon, Santa Barbara Public Library
Eva Mitnick, Los Angeles Public Library
Amy Mockoski, Contra Costa County Library
Sarah Nolan, Corona Public Library
Patrick Remer, Contra Costa County Library
Carine Risley, San Mateo County Libraries
Courtney Saldana, Ontario City Library
Megan Segle, Benicia Public Library
Addie Spanbock, formerly of San Mateo Public Library
Anarda Williams, Burbank Public Library

Funding Acknowledgments

Summer @ Your Library: Explore, Learn, Read, Connect is a program of the California Library Association, supported in whole or in part by the U.S. Institute of Museum and Library Services under the provisions of the Library Services and Technology Act, administered in California by the State Librarian.

Selected California public libraries in the San Francisco Bay Area received support for summer programming in 2015 and 2016 from the 50 Fund, the legacy fund of the San Francisco Bay Area Super Bowl 50 Host Committee, through a signature initiative called The Re(a)d Zone.

The development of the Lunch at the Library program was supported by the David and Lucile Packard Foundation.

California's Summer @ Your Library quality principles and indicators were developed with support from ScholarShare/TIAA-CREF.

INTRODUCTION

*A library in the middle of a community is a cross between
an emergency exit, a life-raft and a festival. They are
cathedrals of the mind, theme parks of the imagination. On
a cold and rainy island they are the only sheltered public
spaces where you are not a consumer, but a citizen instead.*

—CAITLIN MORAN, *Moranthology*

In the summer months, libraries, those vital public spaces, transform dramatically. In California, some of the libraries' "regulars" leave town to visit relatives as far away as Oaxaca, Mexico, or as near as Flagstaff, Arizona. Destination spots like Catalina, Santa Monica, and San Francisco draw families vacationing from all over the state. Homework demands drop off except for students with summer reading lists from their schools. Conscientious high-schoolers look to libraries as venues for completing their community service hours. Library staff put up their bulletin board displays announcing this year's summer reading or summer learning theme. And libraries are abuzz with events and activities. It's that time of year again when children, teens, and recently adults participate in the 100-year-old tradition of summer programming at their libraries.

There are families in which three or even four generations have participated in this summer tradition. It can be a challenge to tinker with such a time-honored and loved activity. In California, we have taken a deliberative approach to transforming summer at our libraries. Librarians who serve a variety of different communities and populations have spent long hours talking about why and how libraries present summer programming, the value their summer programs provide, how they can make positive changes to their programs, and how their programs can stay relevant and have the greatest impact. As a result, they are holding on to the activities that are most meaningful today and letting go of practices that no longer work as well as they used to.

California public library staff are using statewide outcomes to guide and demonstrate the impact of their work. They are using new quality principles and indicators as a means of achieving those outcomes. They are forging new summer partnerships and collaborations, and are developing innovative outreach strategies that extend their programs beyond the library regulars. They are meeting and learning from one another, and forming the beginnings of what we see as an evolving community of practice.

California's public libraries are not alone in making these changes, but the state of California provides an ideal canvas for exploring and illustrating the transformation of summer programming that is taking place across the nation. California is a large and diverse state with summer programs taking place in a wide variety of urban, suburban, and rural communities. Each year over 800,000 children, teens, and adults sign up for summer reading in California's over 1,100 main and branch libraries, and many more participate in over 45,000 events and activities.

As with any story of change, the transformation of California's summer programs is a work in progress. In this book, we present the vision for change that was developed by California library staff and give examples of how California's summer programs are changing. We begin with a historical overview of summer programming in public libraries and a review of the research and conditions that have prompted recent changes in California's summer programs. We then discuss the outcome- and outreach-based evaluation framework and the quality principles and indicators that California librarians have created to help them drive the change they want to see in their libraries and their communities. We review a statewide campaign, Summer Matters, that is working to provide equitable summer learning opportunities for all children in California, and we explore the contributions that public libraries have made to that campaign. And we end with an in-depth look at Lunch at the Library, California's coordinated, outcome-based, public library summer meals project, which is providing free meals for youth in food-insecure families while bringing underserved families to the library, fostering community partnerships, and providing learning opportunities for children, volunteer opportunities for teens, and resources for adults. Throughout, we highlight case studies and observations that illustrate the variety of summer programming taking place today in California's public libraries.

Public library summer programs can transform communities. As we write, California's summer programs are bringing new families to the library. They are providing children with summer learning opportunities, teens with youth development and workforce readiness skills, and adults with lifelong learning opportunities. They are providing hungry youth with meals. And they are nurturing community and connections among people of all ages. We hope that you find useful information here that you can use to transform summer in your own communities. This is more of a how-to-think-about-it book than a how-to-do-it manual. Please share with us stories of your own transformation effort through our website, www.calchallenge.org. Thank you for joining us.

CHAPTER 1

Looking Backward

HE DEFINITIVE HISTORY OF LIBRARY SUMMER READING programs has yet to be written. It is possible, however, to tease out some of the evolving trends and issues by looking at articles published in the library press, mostly accounts of "how we did it good," and at advice and guidance given in handbooks by experts in the field.[1] Many of the elements that are characteristic of library summer programs today can be traced back more than 100 years to early initiatives by innovative children's librarians. This chapter will look back at some of the significant highlights and changes that have occurred over the years to create a service that is now offered in 95 percent of American public libraries.[2]

The Beginnings

The earliest records we have of library summer programs date back to the late nineteenth century. According to Jill Locke, pioneering programs were offered in Cleveland, Ohio, in 1897 and in Hartford, Connecticut, and Pittsburgh, Pennsylvania, in 1898.[3] All three were designed to motivate children to use the library and keep reading during the summer months when they were not in school—objectives that still underpin our twenty-first-century summer programs.

The Library League of Cleveland was designed as a club for young library patrons who would learn how to care properly for books. In addition, the children kept a record of the books they read over the summer and made a list of six or more of the best books they wanted to share with other children. They were encouraged to recruit new members and received badges as a recognition of their efforts. The roster of 3,500 members in the spring of 1897 grew to 12,615 by fall. A culminating program was held in November at the Music Hall, the largest auditorium in Cleveland, where the children sang their league song with its rousing chorus:

> Oh, we are the League, the Library League
> The League ten thousand strong
> And if you value the bright new books
> Join us and sing our song.

In Hartford, children's librarian Carolyn Hewins promoted her program as the Vacation Reading Club, where boys and girls were invited to come to the library once a week for book talks and story reading. Book-lending policies were also changed to allow the children to check out books daily during the summer instead of once a week, as was the practice during the school year.

The Carnegie Library of Pittsburgh used a different service model for its Summer Playground Program. The library provided books and story hours at selected neighborhood playgrounds. Jill Locke quotes one kindergarten child as saying, "I tell you, them skinny books are the daisies."[4]

These three innovative programs were widely reported in the library press, at regional meetings, and at conferences of the American Library Association. It wasn't long before summer programs for children were launched in Cincinnati, New York, Boston, Denver, Detroit, Indianapolis, Seattle, Milwaukee, Dayton, and elsewhere. In 1901, John Cotton Dana added to the national conversation on summer reading in an editorial he wrote advocating that children develop a common knowledge base by reading recommended books.[5] He included a sample list that contained such familiar topics as Aladdin, William Tell, and Robin Hood. At least one public library in Indiana adopted this idea for its 1901 vacation reading club. Each grade was given a checklist of classic children's books, and children were asked to write about the book they enjoyed the most.

Anne Carroll Moore, children's services coordinator at the New York Public Library and one of the most influential of that first generation of children's librarians, wrote about vacation reading in one of the essays reprinted in *My Roads to Childhood*.[6] Writing in the late 1910s, Moore reminisces about her own summer reading as a young girl. She then describes the pleasures books can offer to the New York City kids she serves as a librarian. Specifically, she writes about the value of free reading and talking with children about books they have chosen themselves. "No time is more favorable for such interchange than the rainy morning, the hot afternoon, or the cool night of a summer holiday," she explains.[7] She claims that children see summer reading as a pastime that is as fun as any other in her city, and that boys and girls were outraged when the Health Department closed the library for nearly three months during the summer of 1916, presumably because of the rampant influenza outbreak. She quotes one boy as complaining that first they closed the movies, then the libraries. "They'll be keeping us out of the river next," he grumbled.

Never one to shy away from offering a strong opinion when it came to children's books, Moore had undaunted faith in children's ability to choose good books for themselves, even if that meant skipping the dull parts. She therefore advised parents to let their children choose freely from a large and varied collection of books during the summer, rather than prescribe a course of required reading for them. "This quick sensibility of childhood to great things in life or in literature is too often forgotten by those who would bring them together by a preconceived plan."[8]

Moore does not give any details about how children using the New York Public Library in those early days were encouraged to stumble upon those great things in literature. Presumably they were not provided with lists of recommended books. She writes approvingly of Caroline Hewins's reading clubs and vacation reading hours in Hartford, Connecticut, mentioned previously. She praises Hewins for passing on to children "the rare gift of a companionship with books based on friendship rather than on desire for knowledge."[9] It is likely, based on Moore's philosophy and practice of children's librarianship, that she would rely on informal reading guidance from a knowledgeable librarian who knew how to relate to children.

Libraries continued to adopt summer reading programs after the success of the pioneering efforts was disseminated through journals and conference presentations. An article in *Library Journal* in 1923 referred critically to "the sudden vogue of children's 'reading clubs.'"[10] The author questioned the rationale for summer reading clubs, asking if they were "anything more than half-concealed, perhaps only half-realized, schemes to keep our circulation statistics up over the summer months." While staff at the Chicago Public Library were beginning to question summer reading program incentives, the Minneapolis Public Library reported in the same year that it was beginning its second year of a "summer honor reading contest."[11] These librarians were quick to state that their system did not spoil the spontaneity of reading for pleasure.

The October 1, 1923, issue of *Library Journal* published two editorials on children's summer reading clubs. One supported the use of honor rolls, badges, and certificates as devices borrowed from child psychology to foster children's interest in reading and develop children's wider tastes and a deeper love of books.[12] The author of the more critical editorial worried that libraries were confusing their goals with those of schools and that children participating in such programs would begin to see reading as a task designed to produce an output rather than a joyful experience.[13]

Jill Locke notes that some public libraries reported having to cut back or make adjustments in their summer reading programs during the Great Depression.[14] Portland, Oregon, for example, reported in 1934 that they had no money to buy the usual printed support materials.[15] They improvised by building a castle out of blocks on which children wrote their names and the title of a book they had read. In Charlotte, North Carolina, the library managed to host a party at the end of the summer for children who had completed the reading program.[16]

Programs during the Mid-Twentieth Century

During the years of World War II, many libraries made a special effort to keep children occupied in the summer months while fathers were away and mothers worked in the defense industry.[17] A report of a summer program in 1941 demonstrates another effect of the war.[18] Earlier, this North Dakota library's summer programs had featured international themes, but in 1941 the theme was focused on the United States in a show of nationalistic patriotism.

The Children's Services Division (now the Association for Library Service to Children) of the American Library Association provided a mechanism for children's librarians throughout the United States to network and to learn from each other about approaches to serving young people. At annual and regional conferences and through publications over the years, they developed best practices for such programs and services as preschool storytimes, relationships with schools, and summer reading programs. In 1943 the American Library Association issued *Work with Children in Public Libraries,* an update of a 1930 publication.[19] This new edition reflected current professional concerns about the social aspects of library service to children and the need to work more closely with other child welfare organizations and agencies. It also identified summer reading as a core service.

In 1943, most library summer reading programs were still informal efforts to promote reading during the months when children had more time and leisure. Effie Power suggested that librarians use summer vacation as a time to promote longer books and handbooks on nature subjects. She also warned against using the less busy summer period as a time to catch up on inventory and book repair, noting that this clerical work might spoil the atmosphere in an otherwise attractive children's room. "Summer is the time for leisurely contact with children that leads to deeper understanding of their wants," she wrote.[20]

Themes and more innovative programming were beginning to be part of summer services at some libraries. Power called attention to a procession of balloons carrying titles of books, traveling around the world through reading, building a library using books as bricks, or planning a library garden. Whatever is attempted should be based on children's initiative, planned thoughtfully, and carried to completion. Specific teaching methods followed by teachers during the winter months should be avoided for obvious reasons. Freshness of approach should be the keynote. Recreation through reading was the aim. Other innovations documented by Power were Saturday clubs organized by the children themselves, and library storytimes in playgrounds and parks. She cautions librarians to avoid contests and competitions, adding her voice to the ongoing controversy on this topic.[21]

By the 1940s, educators were citing the results of various standardized reading tests to document the loss of reading skills over the summer and to evaluate strategies for retention. One particularly interesting study was conducted by Ruth Cathlyn Cook over twelve years, beginning in 1940.[22] More than 400 second graders in Mankato, Minnesota, were involved. The Gates Advanced Primary Reading Tests were administered in May and again in September. Four types of summer reading plans were administered during the twelve-year study: reading materials with no work sheets, reading materials with completion exercises, plans using individualized work sheets, and, in 1950 and 1952, library reading plans. The public library's reading plans were similar to many still used today, with children invited to participate for one year in a reading circus and the following year in a reading rodeo. The goal was to read twenty-five books over the summer, at which point the child would receive a certificate.

The results of the twelve-year study showed that participation in any kind of summer reading was better than no reading at all. However, the library reading plans produced the best reading results of any of the four plans. Children improved their reading scores, sometimes dramatically, and the gains persisted into the following January. The author of the study wrote, "If confidences supplied in conferences can be trusted, no summer program for an individual child is superior to one which includes a relaxed child, a good library, a trained librarian, and at least one parent who takes time to listen, to discuss, to supply information, and occasionally to visit the library with the child in search of information or recreation."[23]

By the 1950s, library summer programs had become institutionalized to the point that articles began to appear about how to effectively develop and implement these annual initiatives. Alice Cushman continued to raise the dilemma faced by many librarians: were their summer programs just races to see who could read the most books, or were they designed to teach the fun and importance of reading?[24] She acknowledged the problem of small staffs and inadequate budgets, and she suggested that librarians partner with other agencies such as playgrounds and youth groups to meet the challenge of providing good service with limited resources.

Two Washington state libraries partnered with local public schools for their summer reading programs. Seattle and Walla Walla both worked with teachers and with the PTA to promote the library programs. In Seattle, the children in grades four through eight received their certificates for participation in the summer program at school assemblies. The Walla Walla PTA had a special recognition party to honor the children who had gotten involved in the library's summer program.

Summer Programs in the Late Twentieth Century

One of the authors of this book, Virginia Walter, was working as a children's librarian at the San Francisco Public Library (SFPL) in 1966. By this time, summer reading programs were well-institutionalized at public libraries around the country. The SFPL's offering was typical of those offered at large library systems at that time. Under the leadership of the children's services coordinator, Effie Lee Morris, the library offered an elaborate summer reading program that shared many elements with those at other institutions. At this time, each public library mounted its own summer program. At the SFPL, a committee of children's librarians developed a new theme each year and worked with the staff artists in the library's public relations department to develop the materials that supported the theme. There were book lists, posters, and booklets for children to record their reading. There were no prizes for reaching achievements. However, the names of children who registered were displayed prominently at each library, along with the number of books each child had read. At the end of the summer, a ceremony was held at the municipal auditorium. Certificates were given to each child who completed the required number of books, and children were further honored for their years of participation.

While most libraries continued to include some element of competition in their summer reading programs, there was some pushback. Writing in *The Horn Book* in 1964, Mary Amos McMillan argued against the prevailing structured, competitive summer reading clubs.[25] She cited a child who stopped reading after finishing the tenth book because no credit would be given for reading more than that. In 1993 Alfie Kohn's influential book, *Punished by Rewards: The Trouble with Gold Stars, Incentive Plans, A's, Praise, and Other Bribes*, gave fuel to the arguments of some librarians that external rewards do little to build a lasting reading habit or reading culture.[26]

Herbert Goldhor and John McCrossan entered the debate with their report of an exploratory study on the effects of library summer programs on reading skills.[27] The authors introduced some skepticism about the benefits of summer reading clubs early in their article, reporting other authors who say these programs are among the most controversial activities in the children's library field. Benefits cited include a belief that children develop their reading skills and develop reading interests and good reading habits. Negative effects include the promotion of undesirable competition and the use of these reading clubs as a gimmick to keep up circulation statistics during the summer.[28] Troubled by the lack of reliable research to back up librarians' claims that vacation reading contributes to reading retention, Goldhor and McCrossan undertook their own study. The Evansville, Indiana, public schools administered reading tests to all 1,718 fourth-graders in their 35 elementary schools in the spring of 1962 and again in the fall after the children started fifth grade. Of these children, 135 joined the summer reading club and completed its requirements to read one book from at least 16 of 42 subject categories developed by the librarians. The results of the reading tests showed that children who participated in the summer reading club were, on average, approximately seven months ahead of children who did not participate. However, the authors noted several confounding variables that weaken the causal relationship between library summer reading and reading scores. They encouraged more rigorous research design that would, for example, randomize the selection of children for the experimental group of participants, since self-selection tends to introduce bias.

A study by Barbara Heyns, published in 1975, brought renewed attention to one of the original rationales for library summer reading programs.[29] She was able to document the loss in vocabulary experienced by children over the summer in the city of Atlanta. She found that children from high-income families actually gained vocabulary during the summer months while poor children lost ground. A study done twenty-two years later on children in Baltimore yielded similar results.[30] This study looked at reading comprehension test results. All children, regardless of family income, made progress during the school year. Children in low-income families, however, experienced loss over the summer months.

Most educational experts agree that more reading is what makes the difference. Obviously, reading requires books, and there is evidence that children from poor families have significantly less access to books than those from wealthier homes. One influential study conducted by Stephen Krashen, Courtney Smith, and Rebecca Constantino looked at the availability of books to children in affluent Beverly Hills and low-income Watts, in Los Angeles.[31] Children in these two communities were asked how many books they had in their homes that were available to them to read. The average number in Beverly Hills was 200. In Watts, it was less than one—only 0.4 books per household.

Could library summer reading programs be an effective response to this problem? Alleviating what educators call "summer slide" has always been a major rationale for these summer initiatives in libraries. Some research from the education community has supported the value of voluntary summer reading programs, particularly in helping low-income children catch up to their more affluent peers.[32] One study showed that giving poor children books that they chose themselves at the beginning of summer yielded positive effects on reading achievement that were equal to attending summer school.[33] Other scholars are more skeptical about the value of public libraries' drop-in, voluntary approach to summer reading, however. Harvard professor James Kim, for example, has urged teachers' intervention in order to help lower-achieving children get the most benefit from reading voluntarily over the summer. His studies also showed that children did better when they were exposed to help with reading comprehension strategies.[34]

Jill Locke's PhD dissertation aimed to evaluate the effectiveness of library summer reading programs.[35] She defined a successful program as one that reached more than 8 percent of the child population in its service area. She sent surveys to 500 public libraries throughout the United States and received 200 responses that enabled her to determine the characteristics of successful and unsuccessful programs. By even this limited output measure, only one third of the summer reading progams were effective. The majority lacked goals and objectives, and many lacked any kind of measurement data. Factors that led to success as defined in the study were population size, marketing to schools, and participation of the children's specialist in the design of the program. While this study gave some indication of the relatively narrow reach of library summer reading programs, it gave no data at all about their impact on children's reading losses or gains.

Summer Library Programs in the Twenty-First Century

Fast forward to the twenty-first century. Some things had changed. Libraries were less likely to develop their own theme and create their own artwork, preferring instead to purchase materials from a reliable organization such as iREAD or the Collaborative Summer Library Program. Both offer high-quality resources and products on a new theme each summer. More state library development agencies and state library associations were offering some funding to local libraries that buy in to one of these national summer reading campaigns. In fact, summer library programs are increasingly funded by contributions from local businesses and commercial enterprises. This development has received some pushback from librarians who are concerned about this possible commercialization of a public program. However, few libraries have taken a stand of refusing such sponsorship.[36] The use of trinkets and drawings for more substantial prizes has become commonplace, in spite of the pushback from librarians who argued for the more internal reward that comes from reading itself. The age of participants has expanded from the school-age children of earlier programs to include babies, teens, and adults. The Internet has also become a major component of summer programs, with most libraries having a website that promotes summer reading and learning, many with interactive features.[37]

In Michael Sullivan's guide to the work of contemporary children's librarians, he points out that summer reading programs are now a "collection of programs that run the gamut of program types, but form a special and distinct experience. . . . Summer reading programs encourage reading for fun and in vast quantities, and the goal is fairly universal."[38] However, the need for research that would document and validate claims for the benefits of public libraries' summer reading schemes continued to be cited in the library literature. Joe Matthews made a persuasive pitch in 2010, proposing that librarians focus more on identifying the impact of these programs on the lives of participants than on the more usual quantitative counts of books read.[39]

The Graduate School of Library and Information Science at Dominican University received funding from the Institute of Museum and Library Services to try to resolve the issue of the effectiveness of library summer programs in reducing summer slide. Dominican University partnered with the Colorado State Library Agency and the Texas Library and Archives Commission to oversee the study, which took place between 2006 and 2009. The Center for Summer Learning was hired to conduct the research. Eleven sites from across the United States were selected as participants. All sites had partnership arrangements between the public library and the local public school. The overarching conclusion was that third-grade students who participated in a public library summer reading program scored higher on reading achievements at the beginning of fourth grade than those who did not participate. It was not all good news, however. The participants who showed these higher test results tended to be girls. They tended to be good readers before summer, scoring higher on spring reading tests than other students. They were already library users who had more books in their homes than non-participants. In other words, library summer reading programs did not seem to be reaching the children who could most use the boost.[40]

Even before the Dominican study, there had been concern among some thoughtful practitioners that summer reading had lost its purpose and freshness. Librarians fretted that they saw the same faces during the summer as they did during the school year. Were we guilty of contributing to summer reading loss among the most at-risk children? The County of Los Angeles Public Library hired a consultant to tease out the role of parents in children's participation in summer reading. Not surprisingly, parents who were already highly involved in their children's care and education were most likely to enroll their children in the library's summer reading program. Parents saw the library's program as being primarily, but not exclusively, educational. For parents who chose not to enroll their children in summer reading programs, the reasons included parental discomfort, lack of time or bad timing, and perceived lack of need. Many of the parents expressing their own personal discomfort worried about putting undue pressure on their children or putting them in situations that might make them unhappy. These parents reporting personal discomfort were disproportionately from communities with Families at Risk programs. They were a distinct contrast from the participant parents who enrolled their children even if the latter hated reading.[41]

National Organizations Get Involved in Summer Programs

It was in the context of widespread questioning of the effectiveness of summer programs that the major library and educational associations began to launch their own initiatives to rethink and revitalize this traditional library service.

The Urban Libraries Council (ULC) is a membership organization of leading public library systems in North America. Its mission, according to its website, is to develop initiatives that "strategically advance the value that 21st century libraries provide communities in critical areas such as education/lifelong learning, workforce and economic development, public safety, health and wellness, safety, and environmental sustainability."[42] The ULC has recently partnered with the National Summer Learning Association to focus on the work that public libraries are doing to provide summer learning opportunities. In a "Leadership Brief" that presents some findings from research performed as part of its Accelerate Summer initiative, the ULC pinpoints the assets that public libraries bring to summer learning:[43]

- A trusted, inclusive atmosphere with safe and flexible opportunities to read, create, discover, and explore
- Experience delivering summer reading programs
- Access to and experience using diverse learning resources and approaches
- Deep community connections to support summer learning inside the library, at schools, and other accessible places
- Rapport with parents and families to encourage engagement in their children's summer learning

The "Leadership Brief" goes on to report on nine different public library programs that exemplify innovative and effective approaches to engaging young people in summer learning activities. These include initiatives that expand traditional summer reading programs through more active follow-through, those that implement skill-based drop-in programs, and those that offer focused enrollment programs.

The ULC also offers five strategies for libraries that want to adopt a summer learning approach:

1. Engage team members across the library.
2. Connect summer reading and other library services.
3. Start planning in September.
4. Initiate and cultivate partnerships with schools, museums, and other partners.
5. Plan programming with clear learning goals.

The ULC Accelerate Summer initiative has focused on preliminary research that identifies the models and strategies being used by effective library programs that emphasize learning. One finding of special interest to us in California was the state of evaluation for those programs that aim to generate learning. Initial findings showed that only half of the libraries surveyed were making an effort to measure the efficacy of the learning gained by participants. Sixty percent of the libraries reported that their primary need for additional resources was for assessment. Libraries did note the use of a few assessment tools, including California's outcomes survey.[44]

The Public Library Association (PLA) has also emphasized assessment in its Project Outcome initiative, which began in 2013 with a Performance Measurement Task Force assigned to develop standardized measures that all public libraries could use. By 2015, the PLA had identified seven key service areas for which four patron outcomes—knowledge, confidence, application, and awareness—could be measured. Those seven areas are civic/community engagement, digital learning, economic development, education/lifelong learning, early childhood literacy, job skills, and summer reading.

The PLA outcome tools for summer reading are three simple surveys, intended to measure outcomes for each of three age groups—adult, teen, and child. The children's outcomes are reported by an adult patron or caregiver. Although the PLA's outcomes focus on the traditional reading component of library summer programs, there is an open-ended question on the children's survey that asks the parent or caregiver, "What could the library do to help your child continue to learn more?"[45]

The Young Adult Library Services Association (YALSA) issued its own call to action in 2016. It noted that teens and their families think of the library as a place for summer opportunities. The call urges libraries to expand their focus beyond traditional reading and literacy-focused resources and work instead to help young adults develop the many new literacies and skills they will need for the twenty-first-century workplace. They also call for an increased focus on measuring outcomes and reaching out to the most vulnerable teens in the community.[46]

Summer and out-of-school-time learning were both highlighted in the 2017–2020 Strategic Plan of the Association for Library Service to Children. These linked initiatives appear in two of the three areas outlined in the plan: advocacy as well as learning and development. The plan specifies the creation of a research agenda that includes out-of-school time and summer learning and the development of a toolkit of research-based best practices.[47]

Finally, the Campaign for Grade-Level Reading has championed the role that libraries can play in implementing summer initiatives that are designed for demonstrating impact. At a recent workshop presented by the National Academies of Sciences, Engineering, and Medicine, the campaign's managing director, Ralph Smith, reported on lessons drawn from the previous three years of the campaign. As reported in the workshop proceedings, Smith said:

> Communities can organize to ensure more seamless and coherent transitions from school to summer activities. Summer needs to be more than a plethora of programs from which parents must choose a single program made for part of the day and part of the summer. When schools close for the summer, families still need an institutional anchor. For example, public libraries are ideally situated as omnipresent, ubiquitous institutions, a place that can accommodate a two-generation approach. In those communities where public libraries are seen as the summer successor to school, we're beginning to see a qualitative difference in the relationship with kids and families.[48]

With so many prominent voices calling attention to the role that public libraries can play in addressing the needs of people—especially young people—in the summer months, it is heartening to see that libraries are rising to that challenge.

Tending the Legacy of Library Summer Programs

Those of us working in California to transform summer programming since 2008 feel validated by these recent efforts by national library associations to bring these traditional summer initiatives in line with current thinking about evaluation. We feel that our approach to outcomes measurement is rigorous enough to produce usable data and simple enough for busy librarians to actually implement. We also believe that our emphasis on outreach is an essential statement of the value we place on inclusiveness and diversity.

Our work is funded by the U.S. Institute of Museum and Library Services under the provisions of the Library Services and Technology Act administered in California by the state librarian. We continue to be grateful for this funding, which has enabled the California Library Association to help California librarians design summer reading programs that are based on desired outcomes and outreach to underserved populations.

This book is our effort to document the initiative to transform summer reading in the state of California and to offer a case study in planned change of a statewide library service. We begin that narrative, as we began our change effort, with a kind of community assessment, in this case a look at the state's children and teens with the goal of determining what kind of summer opportunities would be most appropriate and useful for public libraries to offer.

Notes

1. Bertin has compiled a summary of articles about summer reading programs published in *Library Journal, Junior Libraries,* and *School Library Journal* from the late 1890s until 2004 for her master's thesis at the University of North Carolina at Chapel Hill. This thesis, "A History of Youth Summer Reading Programs in Public Libraries" (2004), provides a good starting point for tracing the evolution of summer reading.

2. Carole D. Fiore, *Fiore's Summer Library Reading Program Handbook* (New York: Neal-Schuman, 2005).

3. Jill L. Locke, "Summer Reading Activities—Way Back When," *Journal of Youth Services in Libraries* 6, no. 1 (Fall 1992): 72–78.

4. Ibid.

5. John Cotton Dana, "Things Every One Should Know," *Bulletin of the Iowa Library Commission* 1, no. 3 (July 1901): 33–35.

6. Anne Carroll Moore, *My Roads to Childhood: Views and Reviews of Children's Books* (Boston: Horn Book, 1961).

7. Ibid., 103.

8. Ibid., 107.

9. Ibid., 108.

10. Chicago Public Library, "Reading for Credit," *Library Journal* 48, no. 13 (July 1923): 618.

11. Minneapolis Public Library, "Reading for Credit," *Library Journal* 48, no. 15 (September 1, 1923): 722.

12. Lydia Margaret Barrette, "Children's Reading Clubs: A Wise Plan," *Library Journal* 48, no. 17 (October 1, 1923): 816.

13. Louise P. Latimer, "Children's Reading Clubs: A Regrettable Movement," *Library Journal* 48, no. 17 (October 1, 1923): 816.

14. Jill L. Locke, "The Effectiveness of Summer Reading Programs in Public Libraries in the United States" (PhD dissertation, School of Library and Information Science, University of Pittsburgh, 1988), 14.

15. Bertin, "History," 21.

16. Ibid.

17. Locke, "Effectiveness," 13–24.

18. Kathryn L. Reynolds, "Defending America in the Children's Room: A Summer Reading Plan," *Library Journal* 66, no. 8 (April 15, 1941): 342–44.

19. Effie L. Power, *Work with Children in Public Libraries* (Chicago: American Library Association, 1943).

20. Ibid., 113.

21. Ibid.

22. Ruth Cathlyn Cook, "A Dozen Summer Programs Designed to Promote Retention in Young Children," *Elementary School Journal* 52, no. 7 (March 1952): 412–17.

23. Ibid., 416–17.

24. Alice B. Cushman, "It's a Year 'Round Job," *Library Journal* 78, no. 10 (May 15, 1953): 877–79.

25. Mary Amos McMillan, "No Eleventh Book," *Horn Book Magazine* 40, no. 3 (June 1964): 251–54.

26. Alfie Kohn, *Punished by Rewards: The Trouble with Gold Stars, Incentive Plans, A's, Praise, and Other Bribes* (Boston: Houghton Mifflin, 1993).

27. Herbert Goldhor and John McCrossan, "An Exploratory Study of the Effect of a Public Library Summer Reading Club on Reading Skills," *Library Quarterly* 36, no. 1 (January 1966): 14–24.

28. Ibid., 15.

29. Barbara Heyns, *Summer Learning and the Effects of Schooling* (New York: Academic, 1978).

30. Doris R. Entwisle, Karl L. Alexander, and Linda Steffel Olson, *Children, Schools, and Inequality* (Boulder, CO: Westview, 1997).

31. Fay H. Shin and Stephen D. Krashen, *Summer Reading: Program and Evidence* (Boston: Allyn & Bacon, 2008).

32. Richard L. Allington and Anne McGill-Franzen, "Got Books?" *Educational Leadership* 65, no. 7 (April 2008): 20–23; Anne McGill-Franzen and Richard L. Allington, "Bridging the Summer Reading Gap," *Instructor* 112, no. 8 (June 2003): 17–19.

33. Harris Cooper, Kelly Charlton, Jeff C. Valentine, and Laura Muhlenbruck, "Making the Most of Summer School: A Meta-Analytic and Narrative Review," *Monographs of the Society for Research in Child Development* 65, no. 1 (2000): 1–127.

34. James S. Kim and Thomas G. White, "Scaffolding Voluntary Summer Reading for Children in Grades 3 to 5: An Experimental Study," *Scientific Studies of Reading* 12, no. 1 (2008): 1–23.

35. Locke, "Effectiveness."

36. "Reading Incentive Programs Found to Be 'Highly Commercial,'" *School Library Journal* 41, no. 6 (June 1995): 20.

37. Walter Minkel, "Get with the Program," *School Library Journal* 47, no. 7 (July 2001): 27.

38. Michael Sullivan, *Fundamentals of Children's Services* (Chicago: American Library Association, 2005), 161.

39. Joe Matthews, "Evaluating Summer Reading Programs: Suggested Improvements," *Public Libraries* 49, no. 4 (August 2010): 34–40.

40. Susan Roman and Carole D. Fiore, "Do Public Library Summer Reading Programs Close the Achievement Gap? The Dominican Study," *Children and Libraries* 8, no. 3 (Winter 2010): 27–31.

41. Virginia A. Walter and Penny S. Markey, "Parent Perceptions of a Summer Reading Program," *Journal of Youth Services in Libraries* 11, no. 1 (Fall 1997): 49–65.

42. Urban Libraries Council, "Inspiring Libraries, Transforming Communities," www.urban libraries.org/about-us-pages-13.php.

43. Urban Libraries Council, "Leadership Brief: Libraries Expanding Summer Opportunities," www.urbanlibraries.org/filebin/pdfs/Leadership_Brief_Expanding_Summer.pdf.

44. Ibid.

45. Public Library Association, "Project Outcome: Measuring the True Impact of Public Libraries," www.projectoutcome.org.

46. Beth Yoke, "Adopting a Summer Learning Approach for Increased Impact: A YALSA Position Paper" (Young Adult Library Services Association, April 22, 2016), www.ala.org/yalsa/adopting-summer-learning-approach-increased-impact-yalsa-position-paper.

47. Association for Library Service to Children, "ALSC Strategic Plan" (February 2017), www.ala.org/alsc/aboutalsc/stratplan.

48. National Academies of Sciences, Engineering, and Medicine, "Summertime Opportunities to Promote Healthy Child and Adolescent Development: Proceedings of a Workshop—in Brief" (Washington, DC: National Academies, 2016), doi: 10.17226/24606.

CHAPTER 2

What's up
with Kids Today?

O N JON SCIESZKA'S *SUMMER READING IS KILLING ME!* THE boys in the Time Warp Trio find themselves trapped in a library with the villainous characters from all the books on their school's summer reading list. The leader is a crazed teddy bear. The boys are on their backs, looking up at hundreds of books that are going to crash down and crush them. Jos thinks, "This is it . . . The minute that twisted little bear gives the word, we will be flattened proof of what some kids have always suspected—reading can kill you."[1] Fortunately, a character who is a composite of all of the girls these boys claim to hate to read about helps them find The Book that has inadvertently held the summer reading list, and they escape their fate.

Scieszka's summer reading book is one in a series of zany adventures that take the three friends on trips to other times and places, from the Stone Age to ancient Egypt to the future. Most kids and librarians will recognize some truths—and stereotypes—that are tucked into this fast-paced plot with its tongue-in-cheek humor. Fred would definitely rather spend the summer perfecting his skateboard moves than reading and reporting on boring books. When that girl character saves the day by putting all of the literary villains to sleep with her boring recitations, Sam guesses that she is "all of those girls . . . We never read any of those books. So we couldn't tell one character from another if we had to. She's all of those girl characters rolled into one." How often have we librarians observed that boys are more reluctant readers than girls? And they are particularly reluctant to read about that girl on the prairie, the little women, or any of the characters in the Babysitters' Club, Sweet Valley High, or American Girl series.

Barriers to Children's Participation in Summer Reading

In this chapter, we will take a look at some of the challenges and barriers to young people's participation in libraries' summer reading programs that we have observed and tried to solve. These include changing demographics, seductive new technologies, and the ongoing concern over low reading scores. We have listened to teens and learned about new priorities for summer, including the need to fulfill community service requirements. We have also begun to recruit adults to our summer reading programs, and this has created new opportunities to reach out in innovative ways.

Our learning began at the California Library Association conference in Long Beach in 2007. We reserved a slot in the program and assembled a group of more than fifty youth services librarians to talk about summer in their communities. We learned that summer is the time for some children to visit relatives in places like Louisiana or Mexico. Other librarians in California locations that attract tourists reported a small surge in visitors during the summer. Almost everybody lamented the cutbacks in funding that had almost completely eliminated summer school for elementary school students and greatly reduced offerings in secondary schools. This was especially alarming, given the continuing concern about unsatisfactory reading levels.

We learned that few children come to the library unattended. Even school-age children come with their parents or caregivers. It isn't until the teen years that young people come to the library on their own. In some communities, there are significant barriers to be overcome: lack of public transportation, busy streets to cross, or turf issues created by rival gangs.

Librarians told us that immigrant children continued to make up significant numbers in many communities. They came in large numbers from Mexico, Central America, and China, and in smaller numbers from all parts of the world. They brought with them a welcome diversity in background and outlook, as well as limited English language skills and lower economic status in many cases.

Most of these immigrant families have no experience with a free public library in their home countries. Those who are undocumented often fear the consequences of giving personal information such as their address to a government entity. As we write this book under the new White House administration, fears of Immigration and Customs Enforcement (ICE) raids and subsequent deportation have raised the anxiety levels for these families.

We also heard firsthand accounts of the phenomenon that has been well-documented in various studies of library summer reading participation: the over-representation of children who are regular library users and avid readers. These tend to be children from middle-class homes whose parents encourage them to read and use the library. Children from less well-off families participate less.

By 2007, technology had already become an issue for librarians who wanted to guide children and families in the best use of digital devices and resources. This would grow as a concern over the years as libraries added online components to their summer programs and created programs like San Diego's App Academy and creative maker spaces to give children, teens, and families access to hands-on technology.

There were hints of a division between those librarians who wanted summer to be a time for fun and pleasure reading and those who were looking to provide a more educational or cultural experience. However, for most librarians at that gathering in Long Beach, summertime was all about reading promotion. This was what they felt most parents wanted. Most librarians were using programs with professional entertainers as bait to get children into the library. They also relied on trinkets like pencils and toys to motivate children to read. In some communities, parents were so sold on these incentives that they would actually shop around for the libraries offering the most elaborate prizes.

We have continued this conversation about summer at our libraries with the informal advisory group we have convened once or twice a year since that 2007 conference. We also began to gather supporting documentation about the lives of California children and teens that would inform the development of our new approach to library summer programs.

Here are some of our more significant findings from research centers, child advocacy organizations, and other reputable sources that support the voices of librarians who know their communities well. While librarians are concerned about all aspects of children's well-being, we focus here on demographics and on educational achievement.

The Conditions for Children in California: What the Data Tell Us

We will share data from a number of sources in this chapter. Let's start first with some statistics from the Annie E. Casey Foundation.[2] Their KIDS COUNT Data Center provides snapshot profiles about the economic well-being, education, health, and family and community of children and teens in all fifty states as well as the United States as a whole.

The economic picture from the KIDS COUNT Data Center is particularly grim. In 2012, more than two million California children (24 percent of them) lived in poverty, a situation that had worsened since last tracked in 2005. Thirty-five percent of our children had parents without secure employment, a situation that had become more serious since 2008. Housing costs are a particular problem for California families. Fifty-one percent of California children live in households in which there is a high housing cost burden, compared with 38 percent nationally. This is not a surprising figure to librarians in the state who also pay high percentages of their salaries for housing and who are aware of families in their service areas living in garages and motel rooms. This statistic does not even touch upon the growing problem of homelessness.

While the education statistics reported by the KIDS COUNT Data Center show some improvement in California, they are still not satisfactory. Fifty-three percent of the state's preschool-age children were not attending preschool in the period from 2010 to 2012. Seventy-three percent of fourth-graders were not considered proficient in reading, and 18 percent of high school students did not graduate on time.

The Heller School for Social Policy and Management at Brandeis University tracks diversity data for children.[3] Their statistics confirm what the librarians told us was happening in their communities. The number of white (non-Hispanic) children in California has decreased from 3,287,025 in 2000 to 2,476,553 in 2012. The number of black children has also decreased, from 664,921 to 505,630. At the same time, the number of Hispanic children has increased from 4,050,822 to 4,787,736. Non-Hispanic Asians and Pacific Islanders have increased from 911,662 to 1,024,906. Demographers tell us that the increase in Hispanic and Asian/Pacific Islander children can be traced to two factors: immigration trends and the higher birthrate among Hispanic families. None of these figures alone signals a cause for alarm. Librarians have traditionally been eager to help newcomers, and we welcome diversity. However, additional data indicate that children from Hispanic, black, and American Indian or Alaska Native families have a much higher likelihood of living in poverty than white children, and this is a concern. The poverty rate for Hispanic children in 2008–2012 was 29 percent; 31.3 percent for American Indian and Alaska Native children; 31.6 percent for black children; and 9.7 percent for white kids. This inequality is worrisome.

Ending childhood poverty is one of six policy initiatives of the Children's Defense Fund, one of the major child advocacy organizations in the United States. To further their work in this area, they too collect data. Most relevant to our situation are the state profiles on child poverty that they published in 2015. Their data show that 22.7 percent of California children are poor, with one in eleven children living in extreme poverty at less than half the poverty level. Children of color are more likely to be poor than white children. In 2014 one in three black children, more than three in ten Hispanic children, and nearly three in ten American Indian/Native Alaskan children were poor, compared with one in nine white children.[4] Because we know that poor children are less likely to get involved in library summer reading than middle-class children, these data support our call for outreach to underserved families.

Reading Habits and Reading Levels

Common Sense Media (CSM) is a nonprofit organization whose mission is to provide trustworthy information to help kids and families thrive in a world of digital media and technology. Given this mission, it is understandable that most of their efforts are designed to help adults make their way through the maze of research about digital media. However, in 2014 they published a research brief about children, teens, and reading.[5] The report notes that technology has resulted in a significant turning point in reading habits in America. Nine key findings back up this conclusion:

1. Reading for fun drops off as children get older, and rates among all children have fallen dramatically in recent years. For example, in 1984, 81 percent of nine-year-olds reported reading for pleasure once a week or more. In 2013, that percentage had fallen to 76 percent.
2. Reading scores among young children have improved steadily, but achievement among older teens has stagnated.
3. A significant reading achievement gap continues to persist between white, black, and Hispanic/Latino children.
4. There is also a gender gap in reading time and achievement. As we have noted earlier, girls of all ages read more for pleasure and score higher on tests of reading ability.

5. Reading is still a big part of many children's lives. This points to a phenomenon that many librarians have observed. Once exposed to the pleasures of reading, whether by parents, teachers, or librarians, most children do become avid readers.

6. But many children do not read well or often. Children who struggle with reading find little pleasure in the pastime.

7. Parents' and children's attitudes about electronic reading are still in flux. Some data indicate that children still prefer print reading to e-reading.

8. E-reading has the potential to significantly change the nature of reading for children and families, but its impact is still unknown. More and more families have e-reading devices that could potentially increase their children's access to reading material.

9. Parents can encourage reading by keeping print books in the home, reading themselves, and setting aside time daily for their children to read.[6]

The CSM joins other child advocacy groups in pointing out the persistent gaps in reading achievement in American children living in poverty, particularly children of color. We turn again to research from the Children's Defense Fund in order to understand the connection between education—specifically reading levels—and poverty.[7] The CDF reports that in 2013, 73 percent of California's fourth-grade public school students were unable to read at grade level. This is especially critical because fourth grade is when children are expected to know how to read well enough to master the subject content of the curriculum: history, science, literature, and so on. Children who start to fall behind in their learning in fourth grade because of their undeveloped reading fluency are at risk of never catching up.

The CDF also reminds us that this downward learning spiral is particularly serious for students of color. Their research shows that 87 percent of black fourth-graders could not read at grade level; 84 percent of Hispanic students were also reading below grade level in fourth grade. The consequences of this really show up in high school graduation rates. Only 70 percent of black students and 77 percent of Hispanic students graduated on time in 2012, compared with 82 percent of white students.

The CDF findings are echoed in numerous other studies. It is clear that the underfunded California schools are failing to educate all our children, with poor children of color being the primary victims of this failure. Public libraries cannot compensate for all of the problems of underfunded schools. They can, however, make a special effort to ensure that their summer reading and learning programs target children who are most at risk, and this is what the outreach component of California's summer initiative aims to do.

The Role of Technology

Are digital technology and new media to blame for the decrease in the amount of time children spend reading for pleasure? We know that our children are exposed to digital technology from a very early age.

We turn again to Common Sense Media for data on the rapid proliferation of new media in families with young children. There is evidence that many—perhaps most—young American children are growing up in a media-saturated environment. In the CSM report issued in October 2013, we learn that children's access to mobile media devices had increased dramatically in the previous two years—from 52 percent in 2011 to 75 percent in 2013. There is a large gap between rich and poor children, however. Only 20 percent of lower-income children have a tablet device at home, compared to 65 percent of higher-income children.[8]

The American Academy of Pediatrics (AAP) continues to warn parents to keep their babies away from screens completely and to limit the viewing time of children aged two to five. In 1999 this group issued a policy statement about children's media use. It recommended that pediatricians discourage all television and video viewing by children under the age of two and limit screen time for older children. While television remains the dominant screen medium used by children, new media—cell phones and digital tablets—have become ubiquitous in American families, and the electronics industry is increasingly targeting young children and their parents as key consumers. Therefore, the AAP issued a second policy statement in 2011 titled "Media Use by Children Younger Than 2 Years."[9]

The 2011 AAP policy statement acknowledges that some high-quality programs have educational benefits for children older than two years. However, it points out that the merits of digital media for children younger than two remains unproven. The AAP concludes this 2011 statement by reaffirming that evidence indicates that electronic media have potentially negative effects and no known positive effects for children under the age of two. The AAP also reaffirms its recommendation to discourage media use in this age group. It recommends that pediatricians "explain to parents the importance of unstructured, unplugged play in allowing a child's mind to grow, problem-solve, think innovatively, and develop reasoning skills." Further, it states: "Families should be strongly encouraged to sit down and read to their child to foster their child's cognitive and language development."[10]

In 2016 the AAP revisited the issue with a policy statement, "Media and Young Minds."[11] In this update to its 2011 position, it acknowledges the proliferation of digital technologies such as interactive and mobile media and their use by children on a daily basis. It reiterates its position that children under the age of two need hands-on exploration and social interaction with trusted caregivers much more than they need exposure to screens of any kind. It continues to advise parents and caregivers to avoid digital media use (except video-chatting) in children younger than 18 to 24 months. It acknowledges the possible benefit of using video chat apps such as Skype to communicate with people far away. For children two to five years of age, it recommends limiting screen use to one hour a day of high-quality programming and to sit with the child while the program is on. It reminds parents and caregivers that they can help their young children understand what they are seeing and apply what they learn to the world around them.

The AAP has also issued a policy brief addressing media use by older children.[12] Its research finds that television continues to be the most common broadcast medium. However, three-quarters of all teens own a smartphone, which gives them access to the Internet, streaming TV/videos, and interactive apps. Seventy-six percent of all teens use at least one social media site. Video games are also very popular with school-age children and teens, particularly among boys. The AAP finds some benefits of media use by older children. Media provides exposure to new ideas and information and can provide opportunities for community participation and civic engagement. Social media also have the potential to foster a sense of inclusion among young people who identify as lesbian, gay, bisexual, transgender, questioning, or intersex, giving them a welcoming community.

In addition to these benefits, the AAP does document certain risks from media use. Obesity is tied to excessive sedentary screen time. Media use at bedtime can disrupt sleep. There is also the danger of problematic Internet use. In some cases, children with Internet gaming disorder become obsessed with their online activity and lose interest in "real life" relationships. Cyberbullying presents unique challenges because the perpetrators can remain anonymous. As many as 12 percent of young people ages 10 to 19 are estimated to have engaged in sexting—the electronic transmission of nude or seminude images and sexually explicit text messages.[13]

What is the role of public libraries in this world of burgeoning new media use by children and teens? A 2015 survey published by the Association for Library Service to Children (ALSC) indicated that 71 percent of respondents were using digital devices in a variety of ways in their libraries—with storytimes and public access to tethered devices being the most common ones. Some libraries were circulating devices. Others provide mentoring to parents, caregivers, teachers, and other adults who are making their way through the thicket of conflicting opinions and advice about children's media use.[14]

Some leaders in the field of library service to children are advocating that librarians assume a greater responsibility for media mentoring. They see this role as an extension of children's librarians' traditional role as a guide to parents and caregivers who are looking for the most appropriate books and other media for their children. In 2015 the ALSC Board of Directors adopted a statement, "Media Mentorship in Libraries Serving Youth," which outlines the path that media mentorship might take.[15]

The ALSC statement on media mentorship points out that just giving a child access to digital media is not enough to help that child acquire digital literacy. Digital literacy—a vital component of twenty-first-century education and job skills—requires guided experiences. The authors of the statement encourage joint media engagement, with adults participating in media use alongside their children. Helping caregivers understand the benefits of joint media engagement and helping them feel comfortable with this activity is something that children's librarians can do, just as they recommend good books for family read-alouds and techniques for sharing books with very young children. A more extended discussion of the emerging role of media mentors in libraries, as well as some examples of programs and activities that media mentors have implemented, can be found in *Becoming a Media Mentor: A Guide for Working with Children and Families.*[16]

What About the Grown-Ups?

Much of our effort to transform summer programming in California has focused on reframing the traditional services that libraries have offered to children and teens, moving away from reward-based reading promotion to an outcome-based approach that is both more targeted and more holistic. At the same time, our advisory groups have alerted all of us to the needs of adults for summertime recreation, engagement, and learning.

Some libraries have responded with truly innovative programs that involve adults in new and meaningful ways. In 2016, the Los Angeles Public Library created a game log especially for adults that encouraged them to explore new genres and interests. One of the participants, a thirty-something woman, said that she got a kick out of filling out the game card. It brought back fond memories of childhood summer reading programs. Another participant liked being challenged to try new things. A third woman who had been heavily involved with the library's initiatives for teens said that participating in the summer program reinforced her awareness of the civic value of the library. "It is a way to be directly involved with the services of this fine institution," she said.

Adult summer programming is still relatively new and untested. Children's librarians have a long tradition of summer programs to fall back on—and move away from. Putting on a summer program is expected of them. It is only a small stretch to involve young adult librarians and their teen patrons. Adult services librarians have tended to focus on reference, readers' advisory services, and collection development. Because most adults are not in school, programming for them has not been as seasonal as programming for children and teens. This may still become a robust area for growth. In California, the number of adult participants in Summer @ Your Library has grown from almost 45,000 in 2012 to just under 90,000 in 2016. We can imagine future outreach to adults whose only experience of the library may be dropping off their children to get homework materials, and checking out best-sellers and DVDs. We would love to reach those adults who haven't used the library since they were children, and all those adults to whom the library is an unexplored resource. The sky's the limit.

Implications for Summer Reading and Learning Programs in Libraries

This chapter has documented three areas in which the circumstances of the children and teens we serve are evolving. These children and teens are increasingly multicultural and multiracial and, unfortunately, also increasingly from families that are struggling economically. These children do not read as well or as often as they used to, and they are irresistibly drawn to new media as a means of communication, entertainment, and information. How have libraries and the people behind California's Summer @ Your Library initiative taken these changes into account as they design and implement summer programs?

The overarching theme of California's reimagined Summer @ Your Library is "building community." The hope is that the public library will be a place where people of all ages will find value in coming together to read, discover, and connect. California librarians have found that summertime offers unique opportunities for focusing on these kinds of outcomes. It has become a time when the library staff and the people in their communities can pause and reflect on ways that the library can contribute to their quality of life. Libraries alone cannot build stronger communities, but they can provide resources that people can use to find solutions to local problems. The outcomes and the quality principles discussed in chapter 6 offer some tried-and-true strategies for making this happen.

The outreach component of Summer @ Your Library has pushed libraries to look more closely at their communities in order to identify underserved groups. This has resulted in summer programs for children of migrant workers in Encinitas, for teens in a Sacramento juvenile detention center, and an intensive kindergarten-readiness program for low-income children in East Palo Alto. See chapter 5 for more background and further examples. These are isolated efforts by individual libraries. Lunch at the Library—California's coordinated outreach project that helps public libraries provide children and teens with free summer meals in partnership with the U.S. Department of Agriculture's summer meal program—expands to more California libraries every summer. During the summer of 2016, libraries served 203,000 meals and 60,000 snacks at 139 sites. Chapter 8 gives more information about this development.

The ongoing decrease in reading scores and reading habits among children and teens continues to motivate much of what happens in libraries during the summer. Addressing the problem of "summer slide"—the well-documented loss of reading skills during the time children are out of school—is the rationale for many summer vacation programs. We can count on the library regulars and the children who are avid readers or those whose parents push them to sign up for summer reading, and these kids seem to enjoy keeping track of their reading and earning the rewards that come with reaching targets set by the library, whether it is minutes spent reading or books finished. We hope that our outreach strategies will draw in some children who will develop the reading habit and keep their reading skills alive during the summer.

New media, as noted above, exert a seductive power over children of all ages. Many libraries have turned to commercial or homegrown online programs to enable summer reading and learning participants to register, track their reading, post book reviews, and participate in interactive features. One ten-year-old boy in Los Angeles who was clearly a reluctant participant in his library's summer reading program, said that the online program was the *only* thing he liked about it. His mother winced when he announced this.

While cell phones are now a nearly ubiquitous childhood accessory, computers with high-speed Internet access are less common in lower-income families. Children who might have relied on their schools for Internet access look to their libraries in the summer. The new maker spaces are another draw. Summer can be a time to introduce school-age children to the twenty-first-century skill of coding or to the marvels that can be created with 3-D printers. Couple the maker space movement with good summer STEM or STEAM activities that focus on science, technology, engineering, math, and art and design, and you find libraries that offer something for everyone in the summer, even those reluctant readers that Jon Scieszka writes about in his books about the Time Warp Trio.

In the next chapter, we outline the steps we took to help California public libraries address some of the challenges in their communities and begin their transformation to more relevant and accountable summer program offerings.

Notes

1. Jon Scieszka, *Summer Reading Is Killing Me! The Time Warp Trio 7* (New York: Viking, 1998), 51.

2. Annie E. Casey Foundation, "2015 KIDS COUNT Data Book: State Trends in Child Well-Being" (2015), www.aecf.org/m/resourcedoc/aecf-2015kidscountdatabook-2015 .pdf.

3. Brandeis University, Heller School for Social Policy and Management, "diversity datakids.org California Profile" (2017), www.diversitydatakids.org/data/profile/ 3717/california.

4. Children's Defense Fund, "Children in the States" (2015), www.childrensdefense .org/library/data/state-data-repository/cits/2015/2015-children-in-the-states -complete.pdf.

5. Common Sense Media, "Children, Teens, and Reading: A Common Sense Media Research Brief" (2014), www.commonsensemedia.org/research/children -teens-and-reading.

6. Ibid., 5–7.

7. Children's Defense Fund, "Children."

8. Common Sense Media, "Zero to Eight: Children's Media Use in America 2013" (October 28, 2013), 9–11, www.commonsensemedia.org/research/zero-to-eight-childrens -media-use-in-america-2013.

9. American Academy of Pediatrics, Council on Communications and Media, "Media Use by Children Younger Than 2 Years," *Pediatrics* 128, no. 5 (November 2011): 1040–45, doi: 10.1542/peds.2011–1753.

10. Ibid., 1043.

11. American Academy of Pediatrics, Council on Communications and Media, "Media and Young Minds," *Pediatrics* 138, no. 5 (November 2016): e20162591, doi: 10.1542/ peds.2016–2591.

12. American Academy of Pediatrics, Council on Communications and Media, "Media Use in School-Aged Children and Adolescents," *Pediatrics* 138, no. 5 (November 2016): e20162592, doi: 10.1542/peds.2016–2592.

13. Ibid.

14. Amy Koester, "Young Children, New Media, & Libraries: Survey Results" (Association for Library Service to Children, 2015), www.ala.org/alsc/sites/ala.org.alsc/files/content/ YCNML%20Infographic_0.pdf.

15. Amy Koester, Claudia Haines, Dorothy Stoltz, and Cen Campbell, "Media Mentorship in Libraries Serving Youth" (Association for Library Service to Children, March 11, 2015), www.ala.org/alsc/sites/ala.org.alsc/files/content/Media%20Mentorship%20 in%20Libraries%20Serving%20Youth_FINAL_no%20graphics.pdf.

16. Claudia Haines, Cen Campbell, Chip Donohue, and Association for Library Service to Children, *Becoming a Media Mentor: A Guide for Working with Children and Families* (Chicago: American Library Association, 2016).

CHAPTER 3

A Statewide Approach

THE CALIFORNIA STATE LIBRARY (CSL) SUPPORTS CALIfornia's public library summer programs through a project called Summer @ Your Library: Explore, Learn, Read, Connect. This project provides library staff with a framework and resources to help them plan, present, and evaluate their summer programs. By taking a statewide collaborative approach to the development of outcome statements, quality principles and indicators, outreach initiatives, and other resources, we have created opportunities for statewide dialogue and cooperation and conditions for sustainable change in California's summer programs.

The project name reflects the change we see taking place among California's summer programs. Across the state, library staff are transforming and developing their traditional incentive-based reading programs into innovative learning and enrichment programs that are creating community and connections, facilitating learning and exploration, celebrating reading and literacy, and building strong communities.

The California Library Association (CLA) manages the Summer @ Your Library project. Teams of librarians working in early learning, children's, tween, teen, and adult services advise on the development of its initiatives and resources. And an iREAD California committee advises on the development of theme-based programming support, provides training in theme-based programming, and contributes to the development of iREAD resources. The project is funded by the U.S. Institute of Museum and Library Services under the provisions of the Library Services and Technology Act administered in California by the state librarian.

Just under a decade ago, the Summer @ Your Library project was known as the California Summer Reading Program (CSRP), which focused on providing libraries with theme-based programming ideas and training to help them present their summer programs. There was little in the way of data to allow project staff to assess the project's effectiveness or to develop it as an effective statewide initiative. Nor were there resources to help libraries adapt their programs to the changing needs of their communities, many of which we have outlined in chapter 2. Working with groups of progressive librarians around the state, this book's authors—Natalie Cole, then project manager of the CSRP, and Virginia Walter, consultant to the project—determined that change was needed.

Currently, the Summer @ Your Library project provides California library staff with resources they can draw on to develop and transform their summer programs. These resources include

- an outcome- and outreach-based evaluation framework grounded in the value that summer programming provides to children, teens, adults, families, and communities;
- quality principles and indicators to facilitate improvement in summer programming;
- opportunities to pilot new programming, outreach, and evaluation methods;
- a framework for fostering creativity in summer programs for children;
- training in programming, outreach, and evaluation;
- a statewide framework for developing summer meal programs;
- models to guide participation in local, regional, and statewide collaborative efforts to address summer learning loss;
- a community of practice; and
- theme-based programming resources and artwork in partnership with the Illinois Library Association's iREAD program.

The Summer @ Your Library project both influences the transformation of California's public library summer programs and is influenced by those programs. The resources we provide draw closely on what we learn from California librarians and observe in their libraries. Because California comprises such a wide variety of libraries and communities, the program's resources support libraries at different stages of development and support different types of transformation, including transitioning from traditional summer reading programs into summer learning and youth development programs; moving from output-based evaluation methods to an outcome-based approach; and changing from an inward- to an outward-focused approach that intentionally targets underserved community members and contributes to local, regional, and statewide collective impact initiatives.

To borrow terminology from The Harwood Institute for Public Innovation, California's public library summer community might be described as emerging from a "catalytic" stage and entering a "growth" stage. In other words, libraries are now starting to try new service models. According to Harwood, the "catalytic" stage is defined by taking small steps that might be imperceptible to the majority of people in the community. A limited number of people and organizations begin taking risks, experimenting, and generating results, until those numbers increase and links and networks are built between and among the acting organizations. In the "growth" stage, community members see clearer and more pervasive signs of how the community is changing. Networks are established as a sense of common purpose and direction take deep root. Our goal is for California's public library summer community to progress through the "growth" stage to the "sustain and renew" stage of community life where lessons, insights, and new norms that have emerged over time now pervade the community.[1]

Implementing Change

With hindsight, we can see that our work has aligned with some of the research and theory that have informed change agents in a variety of organizations. We instinctively adopted some of these ideas and adapted them to meet the particular challenges we faced, including working with not one but hundreds of different public library outlets, none of which was responsible to CLA, the state library, or the project. We also had no budget for incentives to motivate participation in the changes being proposed—that is, no carrot and no stick. What we did have, however, was a cohort of exceptionally smart and competent librarians from across the state who were willing to work collaboratively to develop a vision for more effective summer programs that would better meet the needs of the changing circumstances and conditions in California communities.

A typical example of effective organizational change is the Eight-Step Change Model put forth by John P. Kotter in *Leading Change:*[2]

1. Create urgency. Identify potential threats and examine opportunities that could be exploited.
2. Form a powerful coalition. Identify leaders and stakeholders and ask for an emotional commitment from them. Kotter recommends creating a "guiding coalition," formed of volunteers from throughout the organization.
3. Create a vision for change and create a strategy for executing it.
4. Communicate the vision.
5. Remove obstacles. Reward people for making change happen and identify those who are resisting change. Help resisters come around.
6. Create short-term wins. Look for sure-fire projects and reward those who help you meet these targets.
7. Build on the change. Set goals for continuous improvement. Learn from experience.
8. Anchor the change in corporate culture. Tell success stories at every opportunity. Include the change ideals and values when hiring and training new staff and evaluating old ones.

We have no doubt that a big, complex organization that is committed to implementing Kotter's eight-step model would get results. However, the original California Summer Reading Program had only one (and later two) project staff members, plus a consultant. Therefore, the element that turned out to be crucial to transforming summer in California libraries was Kotter's second step, forming a powerful coalition. Groups of reflective practitioners have been meeting at least twice a year since 2008 to advise on strategic program development. They have served as informal action research groups, and they have spread the word about their work and acted as change agents within their own systems. In addition, the state library has been part of the coalition from the start, providing consistent support for advancing change among California's summer programs.

The urgency (Kotter's first step) that helped to motivate the changes in libraries' summer programs was the data on reading skills and poverty, discussed in chapter 2, as well as an increasing awareness—in libraries and beyond—of the impact of summer learning loss on children and teens. Data and dialogue about the impact of the "summer slide" began proliferating and gaining attention alongside the coalition's desire to keep California's summer programs relevant. At the same time, librarians were expressing a stronger desire to expand summer reading to adults to ensure that all members of the community could benefit from programming and engagement during the summer.

Kotter's third step calls for creating a vision and a strategy for change. California's librarians envisioned summer programs that would have a positive demonstrable impact in the community, and a set of resources that would guide their summer program planning, help them create change, and help them demonstrate the impact they knew they were having. They wanted a framework and resources with a clear focus that would be relevant across the state and with a broad scope that would enable them to develop their programs in different ways and meet the differing needs they observe in their communities.

The strategy for achieving this vision has included regular meetings of the action research groups and several years of pilot testing to develop an outcome- and outreach-based planning and evaluation framework, summer program quality principles and indicators, and complementary resources that would resonate in the wide variety of California libraries and in which every library could see itself represented.

The outcome- and outreach-based framework makes community and connections the centerpiece of summer programming—two concepts that are part of all of California's very diverse summer programs. Whether California librarians present summer reading or summer learning programs, whether they offer a summer program, club, or challenge, and whether they focus on technology, the arts, exploration, or one of many other summer themes, they are all working at community development. Our framework brings community and connection to the forefront while helping library staff demonstrate the value of their work.

The quality principles and indicators were designed to help library staff achieve the statewide outcomes and articulate the value of their work, and to foster self-directed reflective practice around summer programming. The principles and indicators highlight the variety of learning, exploration, community-building, and outreach that is taking place in California's libraries during the summer.

Implementation of the outcomes- and outreach-based framework and the quality principles and indicators has been an organic and iterative process. Members of the action research groups were the first to begin using the framework to plan and evaluate their programs; the Summer @ Your Library project then raised awareness of the results achieved in those libraries and the tools we have created. Each year, more libraries choose to use the framework, attend trainings, and access our resources to guide their summer program planning and evaluation processes.

The implementation strategy includes an extensive website that highlights results and outlines techniques for using the outcome- and outreach-based framework and the quality principles effectively. We also provide opportunities for libraries to collaborate on testing programming and outreach methods, and creating models that others can replicate. In 2017, for example, four library jurisdictions were exploring how partnerships with housing authorities can help engage underserved community members with summer programming. A series of workshops have also been conducted statewide, training librarians how to apply the new outcomes and conduct effective outreach. These regional workshops and the annual California Library Association conferences have brought together librarians to learn more and to draw support from each other, making Kotter's fourth step—communication—a reality.

Kotter's fifth step—removing obstacles—has been a lot more difficult to achieve. We realize that local budgets and staffing shortages are major challenges for many libraries. Moreover, the librarians who implement summer programs—and the librarians in our advisory groups—are almost entirely from the middle and lower levels of their bureaucratic organizations. They often have to rely on their own communication and persuasion skills to convince their superiors to adopt changes to a traditional program that may be deeply embedded within their communities. Furthermore, the emphasis on outreach to underserved populations may prompt resistance from more traditionally oriented librarians who feel overwhelmed just serving their current patrons. Despite these obstacles, the number of libraries embracing the outcome- and outreach-based framework and drawing on project resources grows each year.

We are grateful to our action research advisory groups for alerting us to obstacles that we *are* able to change. For example, the original evaluation strategy called for libraries to issue pre- and post-summer surveys to participants. This turned out to be so time-consuming and stressful to administer that one major library dropped out of the project, until we convinced them that we had listened and made changes. We developed a more streamlined approach in which libraries are now asked to administer snapshot surveys as their patrons complete their participation, however "completion" is defined by that library.

Kotter's step six was part of our implementation strategy. We worked at first with libraries that had the desire and capacity to begin using the outcome- and outreach-based framework and, subsequently, the quality principles and indicators. We learned from their experiences and we promoted their successes to others.

As a result, Kotter's seventh step—building on change and learning from experience—has occurred naturally as more and more libraries adopt the framework, develop creative new programs and outreach strategies, and share their innovations. As recently as a decade ago, many if not most summer reading programs in the state were being offered within a framework that had changed little for 100 years. In many libraries, the only observable change was the ever-escalating pressure for more elaborate prizes. California libraries are starting to move from traditional programs, based on external rewards, to a new approach based on reaching out to underserved populations and providing services and programs that cultivate desirable outcomes for participants. We believe this approach to summer programming is on its way to being institutionalized into the culture of California libraries. But even as we hope to one day achieve Kotter's eighth step, we remain alert to any signs that our new, improved, transformative approach to Summer @ Your Library has become as dated as the model we have worked to replace.

Notes

1. Harwood Institute, "We Help Individuals and Organizations Turn Outward," www.theharwoodinstitute.org.

2. John P. Kotter, *Leading Change* (Boston: Harvard Business School Press, 1996).

CHAPTER 4

Identifying Outcomes for Summer Programming

AT THE HEART OF THE SUMMER @ YOUR LIBRARY project is an outcome- and outreach-based framework for engaging people of all ages during the time when traditionally school is out. This framework helps libraries of all sizes create opportunities for the people in their communities to connect with each other and with resources for learning, enjoyment, and personal development.It further recognizes that, for too long, traditional summer reading programs attracted the same people who were regular library users. There is a need to be more intentional about attracting underserved members of the community so they can reap the same benefits as their neighbors.

Our outcome- and outreach-based evaluation framework benefits libraries as well as the communities they serve. Similar to other outcome-based approaches, it helps library staff plan programs that are relevant because they are tailored to achieve outcomes that have been designed with the community in mind. The framework helps to build capacity in the library because staff are learning and practicing the skills of community assessment, outreach, and evaluation. It facilitates more cost-effective programming because time and resources can be focused on designing programs that achieve stated outcomes and engage underserved community members. The framework helps improve management decision-making because results can be used to modify and improve programs that don't meet expectations and extend programs that are proven to have impact. And it helps libraries generate rich and meaningful data that can be used to inform outreach efforts, improve program quality, and demonstrate the transformative effects of public library summer programs. Combined with output data—such as how many books people read, how many activities the library offered, and how many people took part in those activities—the data collected through outcome- and outreach-based programming enables libraries to paint a complete picture of the breadth and impact of their summer programs.

"[The summer program] motivated me to read so I would be a good role model for my kids."

Evaluating the impact of public libraries' summer programs is notoriously challenging because these are typically designed to be informal drop-in programs that are presented on a large scale. Public library summer programs take place over several weeks. Some children, teens, and adults take part in multiple events and activities as well as the reading component. Some simply read. Some volunteer. Some might stop in to one library for programs and activities every now and again; others take part in activities at more than one library.

We know that public libraries' summer programs can provide children and teens with high-quality learning and enrichment opportunities. The Urban Libraries Council has noted that

> "libraries' drop-in and self-directed models of summer learning embody high-quality practices in areas defined in NSLA's Comprehensive Assessment of Summer Programs (CASP). These include inquiry-based learning, shared facilitation, arrival/departure/transition, program spirit, and youth-produced work. Because of strong practices in program design, a young person can often participate in a library's drop-in program at any point and benefit from high-quality programming."[1]

We also know that because public libraries are free and open to all, their summer programs play a valuable role in providing children and teens with accessible opportunities for summer learning and enrichment, as well as providing adults with lifelong learning opportunities.

However, in the absence of any in-depth longitudinal research, it can be challenging to demonstrate the impact of public libraries' summer programs. California's outcome- and outreach-based evaluation framework also helps library staff address this challenge and generate data that demonstrate the value of their programs. Combined with streamlined implementation tools, our framework is designed to generate meaningful and usable results at a time when most library staff do not have the capacity to implement an extensive, in-depth research effort.

In this chapter, we focus on the outcomes piece of our outcome- and outreach-based framework, and in the following chapter we look at summer program outreach.

California's Summer Program Outcomes

The California library community has developed specific outcomes for each age range that participates in the program:

1. Young children and their parents and caregivers, and school-age children, feel part of a community of readers and library users.
2. Teens make connections at the library.
3. Adults find value and enjoyment at the library.

The outcome statements have been tested over a period of years with California librarians.[2] The focus on community and connection is a defining piece of the California story. California's summer programs vary in content and presentation from library to library, but the thread that connects them all is the community and connection they foster and the value and enjoyment they provide for participants. By focusing on these common and critical components of summer programs, our framework has the potential to resonate in all of our public libraries.

Each of our outcome statements builds on research conducted by Dominican University, the data we collected while piloting our outcomes initiative, and observational data from California public libraries—all of which confirm that public libraries' summer reading participants tend to be active and engaged readers who already use libraries.[3]

We wanted to help library staff design programs that strengthen the bond that these people who identify as readers have with their library and with other library users. We are aware that people who come to identify as readers are often those who have found a social setting in which their peers also enjoy reading, or are those who are more introverted and like the escape that reading provides. We wanted them to find a community, and find connections, value, and enjoyment at the public library.

The concepts of community and libraries and reading are very closely linked. Spend time in any library and watch how people young and old interact with this public space. You will see parents reading to young children or playing with them in the Family Place sites popping up all over California. Parents tell us how much they appreciate the library as a safe and comfortable place to bring their children. They see storytimes as opportunities to network with other parents and to increase their sense of belonging to a community. Both parents and caregivers often arrange play dates around their visits to the library.

You will see schoolchildren sharing their homework assignments with classmates who forgot to bring the instructions home with them. Teens may be helping older adults master the new technologies available at the library. People of all ages are fascinated by the opportunities for creativity that maker spaces provide. Patrons chat with clerks at the circulation desk as they check their books in and out. Homeless adults find a place to get in out of the heat or the rain and catch up with some reading. At some libraries, children and teens can now get a free lunch. Even the people sitting quietly by themselves with a book, a magazine, or a laptop in front of them seem to be enjoying the feeling of being part of a community.

This is what we want to encourage through our summer programs. In our complex society, there are many kinds of communities besides the geographic ones in which we live. These communities of choice may be based on religion, voluntarism, hobbies, religion, cultural or leisure activities, or ethnic pride. With the emphasis on community, community-building, and connection that the Summer @ Your Library project has proposed for California's public library summer programs, we are positioning the public library as a significant community of interest that connects people with one another and with resources, and that provides value and enjoyment through its programming.

A Closer Look at the Three Age-Based Outcomes

We now take a closer look at the genesis of each of the three outcome statements, illustrated with case studies and observations from some of California's public library summer programs. The observations were conducted by coauthor Virginia Walter in 2016 as part of an assessment of the impact of California's public library summer programs and to confirm that the outcome- and outreach-based framework is resonant with California's summer library programming. The observations were submitted as a report to the California Library Association in fall 2016.[4]

During the observation period, Walter visited seven libraries in three library jurisdictions: Los Angeles Public Library (Arroyo Seco Branch Library, Silverlake Branch Library, and Watts Branch Library), San Mateo County Libraries

(Atherton Public Library and East Palo Alto Public Library), and San Diego County Library (Encinitas Public Library and Lemon Grove Public Library). The sites were selected for their geographic and demographic diversity, and ninety-one children, teens, parents, and other adults were interviewed. Walter's observations provide rare, qualitative data about public libraries' summer programs and illustrate the community, connection, value, and enjoyment that these programs provide.

Outcome Statement One: Young Children and Their Parents and Caregivers, and School-Age Children, Feel Part of a Community of Readers and Library Users

Most libraries now provide regular opportunities for children from infancy through their preschool years to develop early literacy skills through developmentally appropriate storytimes. Because parents and caregivers are a child's first teachers, public libraries encourage these adults to take an active part in their early childhood programming. Through initiatives like the California State Library's Early Learning with Families and the Public Library Association's Every Child Ready to Read, libraries support parents and caregivers in acquiring the skills they need to ensure that the young children in their charge are ready to read when they start school. Parents and caregivers tell us that their small children like having their game cards filled out when they come to the library. It makes them feel like the "big kids."

Children from six to ten make up the largest number of participants in California's summer programs. This is the age when they are eager to master new skills and knowledge, and the summer reading program or challenge enables them to do this. Many children in the elementary grades like the idea of being part of a group of peers; this is the age when many gravitate to clubs and teams of various kinds. The library can be a place where they feel they belong.

This is also the time when children are acquiring the skills and habits that will determine whether they identify as readers. Libraries can contribute to their development as competent, engaged readers. Those children who don't make the transition to fluency in reading are at risk for mastering subject content which is the focus of curriculum after third grade. Summer is also a critical time in which children without access to books are vulnerable to backsliding, losing the literacy skills they acquired during the school year.[5] Public libraries play an important role in helping children maintain their reading fluency during the summer months when school is not in session. Research on summer reading loss shows that children in high-poverty schools are particularly vulnerable to falling behind in reading achievement during the months they are out of school.[6]

"I get to spend time with my mom & dad reading books."

Observation One: Parents and Caregivers of Young Children

Fourteen parents and caregivers of young children were interviewed during our observation in summer 2016. Of these, only two parents had enrolled their children in the summer reading program at their library. All of them, however, were regular attendees at storytimes and were frequent library visitors during the summer. Most spontaneously offered comments that reflected their appreciation for the feeling of community that the library offered them and the children in their care. Nannies at San Mateo County Libraries' Atherton Library gravitated to other nannies who spoke their mother tongue—Swedish, French, or Spanish. All of the nannies talked about arranging play dates with other nannies that they met at the library.

> "I met all of Brian's play dates here at the library. Sometimes we all go together to the park for a picnic after storytime." (nanny at Atherton)

There were three fathers among the people interviewed. They appreciated the air conditioning; the welcoming, nonjudgmental environment; and the free programming.

> "It's tough here. Everything costs money. Even the beach: there's gas and parking. I can bring the kids to the library for a couple of hours, and it doesn't cost a dime." (father at the San Diego County Library's Lemon Grove Library)

All of the parents and caregivers came frequently to the library with their young children. Storytimes were special, but they also stopped by as often as three or four times a week just to spend time in a child-friendly environment.

> "I don't know what I'd do with Kimmy if we couldn't come to the library. There are no other little kids on our block, and I hate to just take her to places like the grocery store or the mall. At the library, we can read books and play with the toys. I usually just grab a book for myself on the way out." (mother at Atherton)

"Nori loves it here. She loves the librarians. I drive a little farther just to come to this library with the girls." (father at the Los Angeles Public Library's Arroyo Seco Branch Library)

One of the most interesting findings was the pride that many people expressed in their local libraries. The public library seemed to be a landmark in their communities. For parents and caregivers of young children, this was an important reason for their positive evaluation of the library.

"Look at this place. Who wouldn't want to spend time here?" (mother at Encinitas)

CASE STUDY

Oakland Public Library

The children's summer program at the Oakland Public Library focuses on creativity and learning. Summer reading remains the main incentive-based activity because of the high need and demand for reading encouragement in the community. To keep the reading experience connected to children's overall summer experience and sense of fun, children are simply asked to keep track of every *day* they read something; they are not asked to count hours, minutes, or pages or chapters read. Children record their reading on a print or online reading calendar and are rewarded for reading at least twenty days during the summer.

The reading calendar was designed to reach independent readers and, as a result, the library found that most caregivers with younger children assumed it wasn't for them. As a result, the library created a separate board for caregivers and pre-readers. To keep things clear and streamlined, the new board is structured around the same incentive as the children's program, and participants are rewarded for talking, singing, reading, writing, or playing for at least twenty days.

The library connects the children's reading program with engaging library experiences such as open-ended STEM activities, free lunches, and fun performances. The library does the same for caregivers and early learners by providing coloring tables, toys, and programs that encourage talking, singing, reading, writing, and playing—ensuring that early literacy activities are firmly rooted in an enjoyable and supported experience.

Favorite programs for under-fives include animal petting zoos and a musical instrument petting zoo offered by the local symphony, and caregivers appreciate hands-on experiences for their toddlers and preschoolers. In addition, Oakland is piloting Play Cafés—extended and deconstructed storytimes focusing on relationships and play. Ninety minutes long, they encourage caregivers to drop in when they can (many find it a challenge to be "on time" with a toddler for a twenty-minute storytime), and they shift between open play, engaged stories, fingerplays, songs, and a break for lunch. Special toys come out just for Play Café, and in nice weather many of the attendees go outside. Play Café is supported by the David and Lucile Packard Foundation as a "mini-experiment" in serving informal caregivers.

CASE STUDY

Contra Costa County Library's Pleasant Hill Library: STEAM Storytime

In 2016, Contra Costa County Library's Pleasant Hill Library piloted a STEAM storytime program which has become an ongoing hit with pre-readers and their families. This reinvention of storytime didn't require a new storytelling skill set or depart radically from the classic storytime template of books, rhymes, movement, and a craft. The twist came in selecting appropriate STEAM themes, adding some maker activities to match them, and emphasizing the early learning goals the library is after—without getting didactic. Just a few of the successful themes and tactile activities have included the following:

- *Dinosaurs (Paleontology):* Excavate toy dinos or salt dough bones in tubs of sand
- *Weather (Meteorology):* Shaving cream rainclouds
- *Shapes (Geometry):* Make snakes or other critters out of shapes, à la Ehlert
- *Color-Mixing (Art):* Tissue paper mosaics or get messy with fingerpaint
- *Our Bodies (Anatomy):* Cotton swab skeletons or simulated digestion in zip-lock baggie "stomachs"
- *Space (Astronomy and Physics):* Balloon rockets on a zipline

Families regularly express concern about "school readiness" but often do not feel confident about which skills will best prepare their child for the classroom. In 2016, the Center for Childhood Creativity published a summary of research emphasizing the value of early science and math experiences in developing curiosity, conceptual thinking, and higher-order thinking skills, which are indicators of long-term academic success (http://elf2.library.ca.gov/pdf/Library ResourceDocument.pdf). The peer-to-peer and adult-child social interactions that are encouraged by storytimes and post-storytime play have also proven to contribute to school success. By branding STEAM storytimes, the Contra Costa

County Library is making explicit the value of traditional storytime practices and answering the question: "Is my child too young to start learning science?" They say: "Never!"

Observation Two: School-Age Children

School-age children are the primary participants in library summer programs. Interviews were conducted with 29 five- to eight-year-olds and 22 nine- to eleven-year-olds.

With one exception, the children expressed highly positive feelings about reading and their experiences at the library, whether they were participating in the summer reading program activities or not. The one boy who was open about his disdain for reading was a reluctant participant in the Arroyo Seco focus group: his mother made him come.

Children who were registered for the library's summer reading program offered several reasons for their participation. Many said "it was something to do." Some children liked the prizes. Many said they liked the librarians, and children at Arroyo Seco mentioned the librarians' visits to their schools to talk about the summer program.

> *"I got to meet with new people and interact with many kids who came to the library."*

Some liked the opportunity to be rewarded for reading, an activity they enjoy anyway. A boy at Arroyo Seco said, "you could get lots of information from books," and a girl there liked "getting a picture in your head from books."

The librarians are a big draw for children at all of these libraries. Children find them to be friendly and helpful.

"I like how they help you find a book." (girl at Lemon Grove)

Many children (and even more teens) said that not many of their friends were readers, so part of the attraction of the library's summer reading program was the opportunity to be around other children who like to read. One girl at Arroyo Seco said she "got to read to other children during the summer." Children in East Palo Alto talked about why their friends didn't come to the library.

"They think it's boring." (boy at East Palo Alto)

"Kids today are more into technology." (boy at East Palo Alto)

"They don't know about all the stuff there is to do." (girl at Arroyo Seco)

A boy at Arroyo Seco speculated that some mothers (unlike his) didn't make their kids come to the library.

One adjective that came up at every site when children were asked to share words that describe their library was "peaceful." A girl in Lemon Grove said people were "happy" in the library. Children in the Migrant Education Program, a partnership between the County of San Diego Education Department and the Encinitas Library, talked about how beautiful their library was. One boy said, "You can see the ocean from here."

The East Palo Alto Library has an active program of outreach to its low-income community. In summer 2016, the focus was on a "summer camp" for twenty children entering kindergarten in the fall. Meeting daily every morning, the children got breakfast and lunch. In between, they experienced a curriculum designed to inspire curiosity and foster school-readiness skills as well as yoga exercises. A Latino man who has a master's degree in health education headed the program; and he was assisted by five high school student interns, all of whom were participants in enrichment programs at the library throughout their childhoods.

The Migrant Education program at Encinitas is another significant outreach initiative. It is a fact that lack of educational opportunities and poverty exist so close to the luxury homes and affluent lifestyles of so much of this beach community. The parents who were interviewed were not in need of outreach, but they were aware of the role that the library played with low-income families and even homeless people. In some communities, there is resentment of homeless people for taking up space in the public library; this does not seem to be the case in Encinitas.

CASE STUDY

Read Together Summer Reading at Santa Barbara Public Library

The Santa Barbara Public Library's Central Library incorporates sibling and family literacy into its annual summer reading program. Library staff include a special incentive for children who choose to read to or with someone else as part of their summer reading, and almost 1,000 children participate in this social reading component each year—representing 87 percent of the summer reading participants who read at least five books during the summer.

Library staff recruit and train over forty volunteers during the summer to ensure that an adult or teen is always available to engage with children about what they're reading and provide volunteer "reading buddies" to the more than 180 children who request a reading partner.

As a result:

- Library surveys have revealed a 71 percent increase in children reading to others, compared to control data.
- Children act as the home storyteller with almost the same frequency as adults when books are read aloud. Of the young readers who read to other kids, home storytellers were most commonly in grades one through three.
- Reluctant readers reached a five-book goal with nearly the same frequency as average readers.

Staff assessed children's attitude about reading upon sign-up. Twelve percent of participants reported that they did not like to read. Sixty-seven percent of these reluctant readers returned to the program to report their progress, as opposed to 77 percent of all participants. Reluctant readers also participated in social reading slightly more frequently than the larger group. Reluctant readers were represented in every age group, but they were most frequently in grades one and two.

Outcome Statement Two: Teens Make Connections at the Library

Enough research has been done on adolescent development that we now understand that these years of transition from child to adult are critical. The Search Institute has identified a number of building blocks—developmental assets—that help young children from the ages of twelve to eighteen to grow up healthy, caring, and responsible.[7]

The 40 Developmental Assets for Adolescents fall into eight areas—support, empowerment, boundaries and expectations, constructive use of time, commitment to learning, positive values, social competencies, and positive identity. Running through all these is the importance and power of connections. Among the assets that speak directly to the importance of connections are the following:

- Young person receives support from three or more nonparent adults.
- Young person perceives that adults in the community value youth.
- Young people are given useful roles in the community.
- Young person places high value on helping other people.
- Young person has knowledge of and comfort with people of different cultural/racial/ethnic backgrounds.

The public library provides opportunities for teens to develop each of these assets through a relationship with a young adult librarian, through opportunities to participate in teen advisory boards and volunteer activities, and through opportunities and encouragement to engage in activities out in the community. Many libraries rely on teen volunteers to help manage their summer programs for younger children. Summer lunch is a new initiative for libraries in low-income communities, and teens have found this to be a particularly satisfying volunteer opportunity. They often use their summer volunteer hours to satisfy school requirements for community service.

> *"I made new friends and had fun at the events."*

Observation Three: Teens

Of the twenty teens interviewed, only three were formally participating in the summer reading program, filling out the game sheet in order to win prizes. One boy at Watts said he did this in order to get the free school supplies. A fourteen-year-old girl said this was the first time she had signed up for the library summer reading program. She said she liked to read, so it was easy to fill in the squares on her game card. A sixteen-year-old girl said she signed up for something to do.

For the other seventeen teens, the library was indeed a place to make connections. The most frequently mentioned reason for why they used their library in the summer was to accumulate the community service hours required by their high schools. Many acknowledged that in addition to getting this requirement out of the way, they had received other benefits through their volunteer work. A girl who helped with the summer lunch program at Watts said that the lunch service "brought joy to kids who didn't have enough to eat." She also enjoyed getting to know the staff better by working alongside them at lunch. Another lunch volunteer at Watts had just moved to the neighborhood and found that helping with lunch gave her some contacts with other local teens.

"I have friends here now." (teen girl at Watts)

Four of the seven teens interviewed at the East Palo Alto Library were working as paid interns with the library's Summer Camp, a program that registered twenty children who were entering kindergarten in the fall. Using a curriculum designed to foster school-readiness skills, the camp director and the teen interns created a learning community for the children and their parents. These teens had grown up in the library themselves and were graduates of after-school enrichment programs held there. They were all participants in College Track, a program developed by a local nonprofit organization to encourage local teens to go on to four-year colleges. None of these young people had signed up for the traditional summer reading program, but they were intrigued when they heard that participants were eligible for a drawing for a $500 ScholarShare 529 College Savings Plan.[8]

For these East Palo Alto teens, the library was an important part of their civic lives, a place to connect with other college-bound teens and with library staff who cared about them. They were particularly close to Kenny, the camp director. They also seemed aware that they were giving back to their community by providing academic enrichment to children of mostly non-English-speaking, low-income parents.

All of the libraries in the sample had managed to reach out to underserved teens. Eighteen of the teens interviewed were Latino, African American, or Pacific Islanders from low-income communities. Only two teens were from privileged backgrounds. These were volunteers at the Encinitas Branch Library. One of these, a sixteen-year-old boy, liked to read science fiction and fantasy but didn't bother keeping track of his reading for the summer reading program. He appreciated the opportunity to do his community service there, but didn't think the library offered as much to teens as it did to little kids and adults. Indeed, the physical space allocated for teens was much smaller than the children's or adult areas. He had ideas for programs involving game nights that might attract teens if the library wanted to do more for that age group. The seventeen-year-old girl who also volunteers at the library had more appreciation for the programming at the library. She liked the music programs and art shows that were designed for adults.

"The library is more for little kids, but I still love it. The librarians are sweet and nice to talk to." (teen, Encinitas)

Little Free Libraries and Murder Mystery Games at Burbank Public Library

Little Free Libraries

The big project for the Burbank Public Library's teens in summer 2017 was to build, decorate, and locate three "Little Free Library" (LFL) installations in the city of Burbank. The project was planned by the two teen librarians, with approval by the Teen Advisory Board and financing by the Friends of the Library. Kits were purchased for the three LFLs from the Little Free Library nonprofit organization (littlefreelibrary.org). The Burroughs High School woodshop teacher was enlisted to lead and instruct the assembly phase of the structures, and he also built the platforms and posts on which the LFLs would be mounted. The library collaborated with its city Public Works department to find locations and install the libraries.

The project was designed to foster camaraderie and connections among teens and between teens and other community members, and to provide opportunities for teens to learn, exercise new skills, use their creativity, and work toward a shared goal. The teens were solely responsible (with minimal adult direction) for deciding how the LFLs' decorative designs would represent both reading and the library. The project also provided the library with an ongoing opportunity to encourage volunteerism among teens and adults because the Little Free Libraries will require periodic attention for maintenance and restocking with books. Burbank Public Library staff also anticipate that the project, a natural outgrowth of the public library, will have a positive impact on other members of the community as they benefit from more opportunities to access free reading throughout the city.

Murder Mystery Game

Also at Burbank Public Library, the Teen Advisory Board (TAB) planned the finale for the teen summer reading program.

In 2016 TAB members created, wrote, and cast a murder mystery game for all teens signed up for summer reading. The event was held after-hours and library staff gave teens free run of the library for four hours to identify possible weapons, solve clues, interview suspects, and conclude who did it, where, and why! In summer 2016 the murder mystery was "Halftime Horror" and it took place at the "Big Game"; in 2017, inspired by the success of their first program, the TAB wrote a brand-new script, "Body in the Book Shop," in which a mystery writer, paying an author visit to the Scene of the Crime book shop, was first accused of murder and was then, herself, the victim of foul play (all of this acted out by the TAB cast), and the participants were then called upon to solve both mysteries.

By enabling teens to work together to develop the program and then engage their peers with it, the Burbank Public Library is fostering community and providing teens with opportunities to make connections, develop skills, and have fun during the summer. In light of the program's success, the Friends of the Library, in their search for a fundraising event to benefit the library, has invited the TAB members to write a murder mystery for them to use.

CASE STUDY

Oakland Public Library's Teen Summer Passport Program

The Oakland Public Library has deemphasized reading in its summer program for teens. It now awards prizes for community exploration and volunteer efforts—an important change both for the teens who participate in the program and for the library. The emphasis on exploration and volunteerism differentiates the teen program from the summer reading program that teens experienced as children. It serves as a new "rite of passage" for teens instead of a carry-over from the children's program.

The library focuses its Teen Summer Passport Program on community connections, and teens must complete eighteen different activities of varying levels of difficulty to finish the program. Oakland teens have many and varied interests, and library staff provide as many opportunities as possible for them to explore the region's great resources and get credit at their local library. Staff scout out opportunities for teens across the Bay Area, including free museum days, skate parks, farmers' markets, and free or low-cost swimming pools. The Summer Passport Program is guided by teen input, and the library recently added activities such as creating media and print reviews and book lists to meet the needs of younger teens who aren't as mobile as their older peers.

Oakland's program moved to a digital platform in summer 2016, and this change has provided a number of benefits for teens and library staff. Teens enjoy receiving digital badges for participating, and teens from different neighborhoods are connecting with one another through the online program. The program completion rate is much higher than it used to be. And program administration has been streamlined for staff.

To help ensure the program is accessible to all teens, the program is available at all library computers, and in 2017 the library offered a hybrid paper passport as well as offering a fully online program. Staff report that the Teen Summer

Passport Program is truly a great program for teens, meeting them where they are and where they'd like to go!

Outcome Statement Three:
Adults Find Value and Enjoyment at the Library

Adult participation in library summer programming is a relatively new phenomenon—one that is growing in California. Some adults who have discovered summer reading at the library say that it brings back the enjoyment of reading that they had as children. They get a kick out of filling out the game cards while discovering new literary genres. Others tell us that summer is a time for them to do the kind of reading they don't have time for during the rest of the year. Whether they turn to more challenging forms of reading or return to reading for pure pleasure, summer is a special time for adult book lovers. Some adults also report that having a formal relationship with the library through a summer reading program reminds them of the civic value of this institution and their place in keeping that value alive. When summer reading involves an adult component, it can provide opportunities for more in-depth readers' advisory service, increased communication between individual patrons and library staff, and opportunities to demonstrate to adults the value of library services and resources.

Observation Four: Adults

Only one library in the research sample had opened up the summer reading program to adults—the Silverlake Branch of the Los Angeles Public Library. Five women who had registered for summer reading participated in a focus group. One woman was in her early thirties, one was probably in her fifties, and the other three were over sixty. All but one were active in other library initiatives, serving on advisory boards and Friends groups. The branch manager and adult reference librarian had promoted the adult summer reading program in a variety of ways. In addition to approaching likely candidates, they had organized a prominent display of books that met the various requirements on the adult game card.

The five women had varied reactions to their experience with summer reading. One of the older women, a mover and shaker in the Northeast Region

Friends groups, thought it was a little trivial. She would have been happier with a more serious approach, possibly involving discussions of important books. The thirty-something woman who serves on a library advisory board thought it was fun to participate in something she had done as a child.

"I got a kick out of filling out the game card."

All of these women found value and enjoyment at their library, whether or not these benefits resulted from the summer reading program. One woman took the time to send an e-mail after we met to explain how important she felt the library was for creating a positive civic culture. Two of the women admitted that they had fun with summer reading.

"I enjoyed competing with myself."

"The game pushed me to read different genres."

The woman who works with a number of libraries in the Northeast region talked about the multiple ways that library staff supported their communities and worked to deal with the issues that faced them. She particularly admired the work that the libraries do in mentoring teens who don't have the advantages that some other young people do. All of the women praised the quality of the librarians throughout the Los Angeles Public Library system.

"The challenges of reading things I might not have read on my own. I visited a new library and read books. I tried new things."

If any California libraries had succeeded in reaching out to underserved adults—other than parents of children who use their services—they were not part of the sample.

California has seen a significant increase in the number of summer programs for adults in recent years. In 2012, 604 library outlets offered adult summer reading programs; almost 45,000 adults signed up for summer reading and many more took part in just under 9,000 events and activities. By 2016, 911 library outlets were offering adult summer reading programs; just under 90,000 people signed up for summer reading, and many more attended just over 40,000 events and activities.

However, summer programming for adults is still new for many California libraries. The introduction and growth of these programs is part of the transformation that is taking place in California's public libraries during the summer.

Trivia Night at San Mateo Public Library

The San Mateo Public Library offered its first after-hours trivia event for adults twenty-one and over during summer 2016. The two-hour program was held on a Friday evening after the library closed. People arrived in groups until the program was at capacity and, in total, sixty people competed in teams of between two and six people. The quiz comprised forty general knowledge questions and an intermission, and at the end of the night three winning teams received library swag—such as mugs, bags, and hats—along with bragging rights.

The program reflects the library's efforts to engage adults in their twenties and thirties. The San Mateo Public Library offers many programs targeting children, teens, and seniors, but before the trivia quiz program it did not have anything specifically designed to engage younger adults. The library served beer and wine during the event, along with light refreshments—part of the plan to help engage millennials. To limit alcohol consumption, each attendee received two tickets that could be redeemed for a total of two alcoholic beverages. A community partnership with Whole Foods provided many of the beverages and snacks.

This summer program was so popular that the library offered it again in October, with a Halloween theme and questions relating to the 1980s and 1990s, and in February, with a focus on questions about entertainment. The community is enjoying the trivia nights as a fun way to get to know their neighbors and play games in a different type of space. Survey responses have been very positive and have included requests for other similar programs, and the survey has yielded feedback that is being used to improve the existing programs.

The trivia nights are fun for the staff as well as the community—they are different from anything the library has done before, they allow staff to draw on their own interests when planning programs, and they encourage teamwork. Now that the program has proven successful in attracting younger adults to the library, staff plan to focus on promoting other library services and issuing library cards at the events to help facilitate a stronger connection between program attendees and the library.

A Streamlined Approach at Branches of the Santa Barbara Public Library

Solvang and Buellton are both small branch libraries, so the activity from the children's and teen summer reading programs is obvious to all patrons. For years, the branches have wanted to engage adults with summer reading too, and in 2016, encouraged by the Central Library, they were finally able to start an adult reading program—in the simplest way possible.

The libraries did not have a single extra staff minute or a spare place on their counters to manage sign-ups or tracking, so staff had to develop a streamlined solution. Whenever an adult checked out a book, library staff asked if they'd like to fill out a drawing ticket for the adult reading program and drop it into a jar on the counter. And many did! The library used the standard double raffle tickets that come in a roll and invited adults to write their name and either their e-mail address or phone number onto the ticket. Each adult was permitted to submit a total of five drawing tickets during a six-week program period. At the end of the program, the completed tickets provided library staff with statistics on how many patrons took part and how many books they read. The libraries saw almost as many adults in its first adult summer program as teens in the long-standing teen summer program.

Because the libraries started their adult summer programs at the last minute, they were unable to offer a lot of prizes, but they found that the adults were happy to win anything. They were not reading in order to win a coupon for a cupcake, but it was a nice surprise when they did. One woman reported she had never won anything in her life before. The library reported: "We learned that adults need fun. Maybe even more than kids do."

Using California's Summer Outcomes Framework

The Summer @ Your Library project has created an extensive set of tools and resources to help library staff plan and present programs using the outcome- and outreach-based framework. We anticipate that our focus on community and connections will resonate beyond California, and we invite other libraries to adopt our framework and use our tools to guide their own summer programming.

The full set of resources is available from the project website, www.cal challenge.org, and includes

- surveys designed for the parents of early learners, and for children, teens, and adults;
- focus group questions;
- programming ideas to help libraries achieve the outcomes;
- tips on administering surveys and facilitating focus groups;
- resources on community mapping and assessment;
- information on conducting effective outreach; and
- information about using the collected data effectively.

In California, project staff also provide training in outcome- and outreach-based program planning and evaluation; provide technical assistance to libraries; maintain a mentorship program that enables library staff to learn from and support one another; and collect survey responses from libraries, collate libraries' data, and provide library staff with reports of their results. These reports include summary data, charts, graphs, and quotes that can be used easily by libraries. This service helps busy library staff implement an outcomes-based approach and helps them use the data they have collected. It also helps the California Library Association and the California State Library to maintain statewide data on the impact of California's summer programs.

As a result of the framework we have implemented, we know that across the state our public library summer programs are fostering community and connection and providing value and enjoyment.[9] In 2016, children who took part in summer reading

- talked about the books they read (78 percent);
- enjoyed the summer reading (91 percent); and
- planned to return to the library after the summer (90 percent).

Teens and adults who took part in summer reading

- felt welcome at the library (96 percent);
- enjoyed spending time at the library during the summer (93 percent); and
- planned to return to the library after the summer (92 percent).

Outcome-based evaluation is most effective when it is part of a systematic planning process, and we emphasize the importance of staying focused on the program outcomes during program planning and implementation. If you want to achieve your program outcomes, those outcomes must be defined at the start of the planning period, and library staff must develop and provide programs that are designed specifically to achieve those outcomes.

We encourage libraries to set local outcomes as well as implement the statewide outcome statements. We know, for example, that many libraries present programs that are designed to produce positive learning outcomes in addition to fostering community and connection. We also encourage libraries to combine their adoption of the statewide outcomes framework with the Public Library Association's Project Outcome resources. All of the resources we provide help libraries implement the general principles of outcome-based planning and evaluation, as well as helping libraries achieve California's statewide outcomes.

Each of our survey tools comprises a set of questions that generate data about the impact of libraries' summer programs. The surveys can be found in the appendix. Libraries can combine the responses they receive to the survey questions in order to demonstrate that they have fostered community and connections among summer program participants, and show that participants find value and enjoyment at the library. They can also use responses to individual questions to gather quantitative data about the value of their programs. The survey tools are intentionally brief. They are designed to be administered easily during the busy summer period and to allow library staff to add questions that will capture other data that are relevant to their library and demonstrate whether local outcomes were achieved.

We suggest that libraries set goals based on the survey questions. Goals might look something like: 75 percent of children talked about the books they read, 75 percent of teens spent time with other people at the library during the summer, or 75 percent of adults believe the library is valuable to the community. Libraries can use collected data as benchmarks to improve on in the future.

We encourage libraries to gather additional data by holding focus groups with community members. Focus groups generate richer data than can be gathered on a survey or through traditional output-based evaluation methods. Talking to the community is the best way to find out why they do and don't use the library and what they want from the summer program. The Summer @ Your Library focus group questions can be used by library staff as a starting point for developing their own questions that successfully engage people of all ages in conversations around community, connections, and the library's summer program.

Using Collected Data

We encourage libraries to combine their outcomes data with output data, focus group data, photographs (with signed photo releases), and any other information gathered to raise awareness of the value of library services, improve program quality, and provide staff training.

In the aftermath of summer, it is all too easy to move right on to back-to-school visits, fall celebrations, and the many tasks that were set aside during the summer months, and not make best use of the outcomes data that were collected. However, it is very important to make time to let stakeholders know about the impact of the library's summer program. In Sacramento, library staff put summer program data onto the computer screen savers and on flyers that they put up around the library. At an Oakland City Council meeting in 2011, children's librarian Nina Lindsay used summer reading data and research to paint a vivid picture of the potential effects of closing the city's libraries. Her appeal was part of a massive mobilization effort that ended up averting the proposed library closures.

Outcomes data should also be used to strengthen programs that are going well and to change or stop doing things that aren't working. They should be set as benchmark data to improve on in future years. And they should be used as a starting point for reflective practice and for thinking about why the library offers summer programs and the desired results and impact we want to see. We recommend not worrying about the things that didn't go well. Any lessons learned can be used to make the program better in the future. It is most important to keep staff engaged with the process so they can improve their skills and their programs year after year.

Looking Forward

Eight libraries participated in the first year of our pilot outcomes project in 2008. In 2016, thirty-six public library jurisdictions used the Summer @ Your Library outcomes framework and over 14,000 children, teens, and adults completed program surveys. Participating librarians tell us about the benefits they've derived from developing outcomes-based summer reading programs:

> "The purposefulness of creating a community of readers helped greatly in making tough decisions about programming in our small and short-staffed library."

"Focus groups gave tons of insight about what to do and how to communicate better with children and teens."

By encouraging libraries to present outcome-based summer reading programs, and to plan, present, and evaluate their programs within the Summer @ Your Library outcome- and outreach-based framework, we are asking for a culture shift in libraries, and we know it will take time to facilitate outcome- and outreach-based summer programming fully throughout the state. However, at times of limited resources, we all need to target our resources to community need and demonstrate the results of our efforts. Presenting outcome- and outreach-based programs is the way to do this.

Notes

1. Urban Libraries Council, "Accelerate Summer," www.urbanlibraries.org/accelerate-summer-initial-findings-pages-450.php.

2. The early stages of the development of the outcomes framework were reported in Natalie Cole, Virginia Walter, and Eva Mitnick, "Outcomes + Outreach: The California Summer Reading Outcomes Initiative," *Public Libraries* 52, no. 2 (March/April 2013): 38–43.

3. Susan Roman, Deborah T. Carran, and Carole D. Fiore, "The Dominican Study: Public Library Summer Reading Programs Close the Reading Gap" (River Forest, IL: Graduate School of Library & Information Science, Dominican University, June 2010), www.oregon.gov/osl/LD/youthsvcs/srp.certificates/dominicanstudy.pdf.

4. Virginia A. Walter, "Summer Reading Research Report" (report submitted to the California Library Association, September 2016).

5. Fay H. Shin and Stephen D. Krashen, *Summer Reading: Program and Evidence* (Boston: Allyn & Bacon, 2008), xi.

6. Richard L. Allington and Anne McGill-Franzen, "Summer Reading Loss," in *Summer Reading: Closing the Rich/Poor Reading Achievement Gap* (New York: Teachers College Press, 2012), 1–19.

7. Search Institute, "40 Developmental Assets for Adolescents," www.search-institute.org/content/40-developmental-assets-adolescents-ages-12–18.

8. ScholarShare College Savings Plan, "'Read for the Win' Sweepstakes: Official Rules" (2016), www.scholarshare.com/documents/ScholarShare-Summer-Reading-Sweepstakes-Rules-2016.pdf.

9. California Library Association, "Summer @ Your Library: Explore, Learn, Read, Connect," http://calchallenge.org/impact/.

CHAPTER 5

Reaching Out

And so the moment that we persuade a child, any child, to cross that threshold into a library, we've changed their lives forever, and for the better. This is an enormous force for good. —*BARACK OBAMA*[1]

THE THREE AGE-BASED OUTCOMES IDENTIFIED BY CALIfornia librarians for the Summer @ Your Library evaluation framework, and the case studies and observations included in the previous chapter, are good reminders of the benefits that public libraries' summer programs can bring to people who participate in them. However, as we noted previously, both anecdotal evidence and research studies have shown that summer reading participants tend to be regular library users, and children, teens, and adults who are already capable readers who are motivated to read.[2] Just as these findings contributed to our focus on community and connection, they also inspired us to develop an inclusive framework that would help California librarians challenge themselves to identify target groups of underserved children, teens, adults, or families who have not traditionally participated in the library's summer programming, and to devise strategies for bringing them into the library—or for bringing the library to them.

By bringing more underserved people into the library as regular users of our services, we contribute to building better communities. We know that children who read during the summer are less likely to lose their reading skills during the vacation months. Children and teens who take part in summer learning and enrichment activities are less likely to experience summer learning loss. We know the valuable role that the library plays for adults as a hub for civic engagement and community connections. And we understand the importance for families to be able to draw on a web of community supports in order to engage in the increasingly challenging task of raising healthy kids. Public library summer programs have the potential to draw people of all ages into that web so they can be nurtured by it and be enabled to nurture others as well.

By providing an outcome- *and* outreach-based planning and evaluation framework, the Summer @ Your Library project helps library staff demonstrate the value of their summer programs, and it helps to ensure that these programs fulfill their potential by providing opportunities for everyone to find community, connection, value, and enjoyment at the library. We are deeply committed to reaching out to those members of our community who have not yet found their way to our libraries. Our outcome- and outreach-based initiative is intended to institutionalize our ongoing efforts to open our hearts and minds and doors to every man, woman, and child in our service areas.

The Need for Effective Outreach during the Summer

In the most recent comprehensive study of public libraries' summer reading programs, the Dominican Study, conducted between 2006 and 2009, students who took part in summer reading reported that they enjoyed reading books and going to the library. In addition, parents reported that their children who took part in summer reading spent more time reading over the summer and read more books, were better prepared for school in the fall, and read more confidently. However, the Dominican Study also found that students who participated in summer reading were of a higher socioeconomic status than those who did not participate, the group comprised more females and more white students, and participating students had more books in their homes than non-participating students.[3]

More recently, the 2017 Scholastic Kids and Family Reading Report has found that teens and boys are less likely to enjoy summer reading than children and girls, and teens are less likely than younger children to believe in the value of reading. Scholastic reports:

> "When it comes to children's views on summer reading, common patterns in reading attitudes persist. Enjoyment of summer reading is highest among younger children and girls, dropping as age increases and among boys."[4]

As children grow older, their belief that reading books in the summer will help them during the school year decreases along with their enjoyment of summer reading—88 percent of children ages six to eight believe that reading books will help them during the school year, compared with 75 percent of teens ages twelve to fourteen and 73 percent of teens ages fifteen to seventeen.[5] These data reflect summer reading participation patterns in California. Of the 800,000 people who signed up for summer reading in California in 2016, just over 614,000 were children and early learners, a little over 97,000 were teens, and just over 89,000 were adults.[6]

The Scholastic report also highlights differences in knowledge and behavior around summer reading between higher and lower-income families. The report notes that

"on average, kids read 8 books over the summer, but this varies widely by age, with … one in five 12–17 year-olds and one in five kids from lower-income families not reading any books at all."[7]

Correspondingly, while 48 percent of parents surveyed by Scholastic reported that they had heard about summer slide, only 38 percent of the lowest-income families reported hearing about it, compared with 59 percent of the highest-income families.[8]

In a call to action, the authors of the Dominican Study appealed for librarians to

"work with teachers and school librarians to identify non-readers and under-performing students and to reach out to those students in order to engage them in library activities."[9]

Similarly, YALSA has called for libraries to

"make a commitment to reach out to and serve the most vulnerable youth in their communities and address their needs, whatever they may be, such as opportunities to gain English language skills, the chance to participate in the USDA's Summer Food Service Program, or having a safe space to go to."[10]

Our call to action broadens these appeals and asks library staff to identify, reach out to, and engage community members of all ages who are currently underserved by the library and who might benefit the most from its summer programs.

Of course, library staff face very real challenges that can serve as barriers to effective outreach. In understaffed libraries, it is difficult to find time to leave the desk and the building and go out into the community. Some staff are not comfortable or skilled in making connections with individuals and groups they do not know and with whom they are unfamiliar. During the busy summer planning and implementation period, it can seem to take all of everyone's time just to plan and offer programs for the library's "destination visitors"—those children, teens, and adults who choose to visit during the summer.

However, we know that public libraries' summer programs can provide tremendous benefits for the people who participate in them. They foster community and connection and provide value and enjoyment for participants. Reading incentive programs encourage children, teens, and adults to read—and be read to—during the summer months. Learning and enrichment programs extend the reading experience and provide teens with youth development opportunities that can help them develop social-emotional and workforce readiness skills. Programming for adults provides them with lifelong learning opportunities and connects them with vital services and resources that are available free of charge, year-round, at the library.

To truly fulfill the public library's potential during the summer months, staff must identify and reach out to underserved community members and engage them with programs that are designed to align with their aspirations and meet their needs. Summer at the library showcases the very best of what a library can be—a vibrant and energized community hub providing essential programs, resources, and services. We must engage our underserved communities with the library during the summer and give them access to all the benefits that the public library's summer programs can provide.

Resources

Led by the California Library Association, the Summer @ Your Library project presents an annual One Million Readers Challenge to increase summer reading participation in California. Libraries that sign up for the challenge commit to increasing their efforts to engage their communities with summer reading. Organizations such as the California State Parks, Campaign for Grade-Level Reading, California State Library, and California Association of Museums have all signed on to help raise awareness of summer reading. Librarians share tips on the Summer @ Your Library website on engaging community partners and creating a buzz around summer. And library directors issue local challenges to increase their participation numbers: in 2016 library director Derek Wolfgram dyed his hair with pink, purple, and blue polka dots when the Redwood City Public Library reached its summer reading goal.

Summer Reading at the California State Library

The California State Library supports and promotes the One Million Readers Challenge with its own in-house summer reading program. In 2016, 234 readers, mostly state employees, read a total of 1,530 books, and the top three readers were awarded with plaques. All participants were entered into a random drawing and three lucky winners each received a California State Parks Historian Passport, an annual pass that allows unlimited entry to many of the state's historic parks. The State Library promoted the challenge to state public information officers and legislative staff and on social media sites throughout the summer. The program, which has been featured in the *Sacramento Bee*'s "State Worker" column, not only highlights the State Library's support for summer reading, it also encourages adults to read and provides a model for other workplace-based reading programs.

State and local challenges are a great way to generate enthusiasm around efforts to increase summer reading participation. However, appeals to the community at large must be paired with more focused outreach efforts that identify and reach out intentionally to children, teens, adults, and families who are not finding their way to the library during the summer, to people and groups who are currently underserved by the library, and to those who might benefit the most from the library's programs and services.

To help California library staff implement targeted outreach efforts, the Summer @ Your Library project provides in-person training for library staff and has made available online a set of resources to help libraries create community partnerships, conduct community needs assessment, and identify underserved groups.

We encourage librarians to engage in a systematic effort to analyze the demographics in their community before planning their summer programs. The goal is to bring together data sources such as census reports and educational statistics such as local reading scores with more qualitative data from observations, interviews with key informants, and focus groups. Librarians learn how to glean local knowledge from people who live in the community and use that knowledge to inform their own professional standards and experiences.

We remind staff that if they want to bring underserved community members to the library, they must tailor their programs and services to the people they want to engage. Talk to members of the targeted group and to their trusted stakeholders to find out what their aspirations and needs are. Talk about what they want and need from the library. Use collected data to design programs, services, and resources that will be meaningful and will ensure that the library is appealing and relevant to the targeted group.

It is important to stay on the lookout for resources that can provide new outreach ideas. Each year, the iREAD Resource Guide includes resources to support outreach and program promotion that are tailored to its summer reading theme. YALSA's *The Complete Summer Reading Program Manual from Planning to Evaluation* includes chapters on collaboration, partnership and marketing, promotion, and outreach.[11] Professional conferences, institutes, discussion lists, and Facebook groups are great places to learn from colleagues about successes and lessons learned. You never know where the next great tip or idea might come from.

The California Library Association and the California State Library have established statewide partnerships and programs that help libraries implement outreach-based summer programs. California's statewide Summer Matters campaign, which is discussed in chapter 7, brings together educators, elected officials, public agencies, and program providers to expand and improve access to high-quality summer learning opportunities for California students. In southern California, a Greater Los Angeles Summer Network, an offshoot of the statewide campaign, now meets regularly, bringing together educators, policy makers, funders, program providers, and librarians. The Lunch at the Library program featured in chapter 8 helps libraries establish successful, outreach-based summer meal programs that connect new families with summer reading. And the State Library's Harwood Public Innovation for California's Public Libraries project, which is funded by the U.S. Institute of Museum and Library Services under the provisions of the Library Services and Technology Act administered in California by the state librarian, is helping library staff use The Harwood Institute's framework to change the way they and their libraries work, make more intentional judgements and choices in creating change, and have greater impact and relevance in the community. These initiatives are providing an impetus for new partnerships and programs and are models for successful community engagement.

It is important to set realistic goals for the library's outreach efforts, especially if library staff are not experienced in doing outreach during the summer. We encourage libraries not to target large numbers for new groups; in some cases, it might be as small as "five teen mothers" or "ten children from the homeless shelter" in the first year. It can be very effective to target just a few people and then use the results achieved in the first year as benchmark data to improve on the following year. The important thing is that a relationship is started and then continued. We encourage libraries to maintain the relationships they start during the summer and continue focusing outreach efforts on their targeted underserved groups until they have an ongoing and meaningful relationship with group members and the group is no longer considered underserved.

Outreach-Based Summer Programs in California's Public Libraries

California public libraries have used the Summer @ Your Library framework and resources to engage a variety of underserved community groups with their summer programming. Just a few examples include children living in homeless shelters, teens in a residential drug facility, parents and preschoolers at a local child care center, homeless patrons, members of the Boys and Girls Club, food bank recipients, teen mothers and fathers, the children of non-English speakers, LGBT teens, and children living in domestic violence shelters.

Both the Sacramento Public Library and the Los Angeles Public Library have used the outcome- and outreach-based framework to encourage branch staff to identify groups who are underserved in their communities and then design and offer programs that are tailored to appeal to the people in those groups.

CASE STUDY

Sacramento Public Library

The Sacramento Public Library initiated several outreach efforts as part of its summer programming in 2011.

Central Library staff formed a partnership with the Sacramento Youth Detention Facility (YDF). Over 60 teens at the facility participated in the summer reading program and 24 completed it. All teens received books that aligned with their interests and reading levels as prizes for participating. When the public library's outreach efforts started, the youth detention facility only had a rudimentary library; as a result of the summer partnership, the public library began providing donated books for the facility's library. The library is now in its third year of providing a customized summer reading opportunity for YDF residents. They receive a custom activity sheet with learning activities that are aligned with their program and the materials they can access in the facility. Moreover, the summer outreach has led to a partnership between the YDF and the Friends of the Library, who have provided funding for a deposit collection of high-interest reading materials so that the residents have access to attractive and motivating reading materials.

One of Sacramento's smallest libraries, the Courtland Branch Library, is located in a town of 695 people, and the library serves a rural population comprising mostly Spanish-speaking migrant and non-migrant families. The library's single staff person formed a partnership to make certain that all youths and adults who participated at the YMCA during the summer also completed the library's summer reading program. The librarian performed multiple storytimes, programs, and library instruction sessions at the YMCA, and by the end of summer, over 47 percent of the Courtland community had participated in summer reading.

One of Sacramento's urban libraries, the Southgate Branch Library, is in one of the county's most economically challenged areas. The majority of children are eligible for free or reduced-price school lunches, and 5,000 children under the age of five live within a five-mile radius of the library. The children's librarian launched one of the system's most ambitious outreach efforts, targeting the large pre-reader population in her service area through partnerships with Head Start groups. The partnerships engaged previously underserved children, families, and teachers with summer reading, and Head Starts used their library visits to begin school readiness preparation for their students. The children's librarian cites a partnership with the Crossroad Gardens Head Start as the most successful: "Ninety sign-ups and ninety finishers. This includes several family members of the teachers. As a group, the pre-readers attended fifteen library programs between June and August. The teachers are modeling for the parents by showing them the library is an important part of family life."

CASE STUDY

Los Angeles Public Library

The Los Angeles Public Library (LAPL) began using the Summer @ Your Library outcome- and outreach-based framework in 2011. In order to reach children, teens, and families who were not using the library, children's and young adult librarians in each of the LAPL's seventy-two branches and Central Library were asked to

1. identify a group in their communities that was not currently participating in the library's summer reading program; some groups chosen included Chinese-speaking families, children at a particular elementary school, families from a local housing project, teen boys, and so on;
2. set a goal of how many members of that group would participate in the 2011 summer reading program; this ranged from as few as five to as many as forty; and
3. describe what outreach and programming they would do to achieve this goal; the point being that in order to achieve their goal, librarians would have to make an intentional change in the way they had been planning and implementing their summer programs in the past.

At the end of the summer, librarians reported on how well they had been able to achieve their goal and what was particularly successful (or unsuccessful) about their approach. The emphasis was not so much on the goal itself as on the experience of doing targeted outreach and making needed changes to the summer reading program itself.

Although this is a simple concept, in practice it has taken several years to really take hold. That first summer, few members of the library staff actually changed their summer reading program to attract and appeal to their targeted group. For example, many librarians chose boys as their targeted group, but only one actually changed her activities to have more boy appeal (she offered Xbox 360, duct tape crafts, and bought and promoted more books for boys). While this is still problematic, over the years LAPL librarians have become accustomed to planning a summer reading program that meets the needs of the community they are trying to serve.

The biggest and most positive change that has come about over the years is that LAPL librarians now take it as a given that summer at the library is not just for the kids, teens, and families who use the library all the time. Summer is now seen as a time to go out into the community, both before summer to promote it and also during summer to actually bring the summer program to kids, teens, and families wherever they might be—parks, day care centers, community centers, and public housing. Getting out of the library before and during summer is now an essential activity, and as a result they are reaching more people than ever before.

Other California libraries are also presenting summer programs that are intentionally designed to connect one or more underserved groups with the library and its summer programs.

Year of STEAM at Contra Costa County Library

2016 was the "Year of STEAM" at the Contra Costa County Library. To celebrate, the library launched a brand-new summer program in its twenty-six community libraries. In previous years, the summer program focused on reading; but in 2016 the library rethought its approach, invested in toys and gadgets, and added science, technology, engineering, art and design, and math (STEAM) activities. Libraries offered weekly challenges that could be picked up and completed at home, including opportunities for families to try new skills like writing their names in code, building balloon rockets, and identifying backyard bugs. The baby summer reading program included activities designed to foster the practicing of early literacy skills along with easy and fun STEAM learning. Babies were encouraged to blow bubbles, build with blocks and knock them down, play in the dirt, and look at the moon.

Summer of STEAM went on tour with outreach programming in schools, housing authority neighborhoods, and First Five Centers. At the Concord First Five Center, library staff set up multiple stations for kids and families to together enjoy using the library's new STEAM toys. Kids could build with DUPLO® blocks, use magnets to find metal items hidden in large tubs of rice, and plant indoor greenhouses. The room was filled with preschoolers and their adults enjoying the experience of discovering and experimenting together, and everyone left with a free book and a baby summer reading log. At the Bay Point First Five Center, library staff gave a presentation to parents about the importance of getting library cards, participating in summer reading, and engaging in early literacy and STEAM play with their children.

Summer of STEAM was a success with young children and their caregivers. Families visited the library, celebrated reading, and engaged in STEAM play together, and the library saw an increase in summer program participation by both babies and adults.

Buena Park Library District's Pop-Up Library

Several years ago, in Buena Park, California, a kindergarten teacher, Mrs. Milch, began visiting a local park to read stories to a small group of children from her elementary school. She started reading in the park because many of the school-children had limited transportation and little or no access to books during the summer. She brought along fruit from a local nonprofit organization, Giving Children Hope, so the children could enjoy healthy snacks while they listened. She promoted her club with flyers that read, "Come read with Mrs. Milch."

In 2014, library staff teamed up with Mrs. Milch to sign up the children for summer reading. To attract attention, they hung a banner welcoming every-one to the Buena Park Pop-Up Library. The partnership and the Pop-Up Library began simply, with a library clerk driving donated books to the park in her per-sonal van. She and two colleagues used the honor system to check out books, and the return rate was over 90 percent. Children tracked their reading on book logs and returned to the park each Wednesday to pick up reading prizes. On the last day of the Pop-Up Library, each child selected five books to take home and keep. The library also partnered with Successful Families of Buena Park, a par-ent group sponsored by the Community Action Partnership of Orange County, who set up a table and provided information to parents about healthy eating. By 2016, 173 children were coming to the park each week, and more than 1,900 books were checked out over the course of the summer.

Mrs. Milch's reading club gave library staff an opportunity to engage families and prompted staff to increase their outreach efforts. The library has since pur-chased a small van to use for outreach and has expanded summer reading to an additional school location. Library staff provide tours for parents who are part of Successful Families of Buena Park, many of whom would not have come to the library had it not been for the Pop-Up Library. The library's outreach efforts continue throughout the year, and library staff now receive numerous invita-tions to attend city and school events. The Pop-Up Library not only engaged new families with summer reading, it also raised the library's profile among the Buena Park community.

CASE STUDY

Outreach to Middle-Schoolers at Benicia Public Library

The Benicia Public Library's children's summer reading program is designed for children ages zero to thirteen, but library staff have observed a sharp drop-off in sign-ups and participation after kids reach the age of ten. In 2016, the library created a special set of events specifically targeting middle-schoolers, and it strictly limited attendance at those events to that age group. Most of the events, such as terrarium-making and T-shirt upcycling, were hands-on. The library partnered with NorCal Bats, an agency dedicated to the rescue, rehabilitation, and release of bats, for a kickoff event, and with the Benicia Makerspace for an activity allowing middle-schoolers to take apart electronics.

The hands-on and interactive events gave library staff opportunities to forge connections with the middle-schoolers; now, when staff see them in the library, they know the middle-schoolers by name, and the children appreciate the special attention. As a bonus, the events enabled students from Benicia's four elementary schools, and even a few new students, to meet and interact before starting middle school in the fall. At the end of the summer, library staff discovered that summer reading participation by middle-schoolers had risen 41 percent.

An increased focus on targeted community outreach is a significant part of the transformation we are seeing among California's public library summer programs. However, we know we are still a long way from engaging all—or even the majority—of California's underserved communities, and we will continue to support library staff in their efforts to develop programs that are designed to reach and engage everyone. In the next chapter, we look at the quality principles and indicators that California's library community has developed to guide summer programming and that we anticipate will prove effective in helping library staff reach out intentionally beyond the summer regulars.

Notes

1. From a speech on "Literacy and Education in a 21st-Century Economy," given by Barack Obama at the annual conference of the American Library Association, June 25, 2005, available at http://obamaspeeches.com/024-Literacy-and-Education-in-a-21st-Century-Economy-Obama-Speech.htm.

2. See, for example, Laura M. Justice, Shayne B. Piasta, Janet L. Capps, Stephanie R. Levitt, and Columbus Metropolitan Library, "Library-Based Summer Reading Clubs: Who Participates and Why?" *Library Quarterly: Information, Community, Policy* 83, no. 4 (October 2013): 321–40.

3. Susan Roman, Deborah T. Carran, and Carole D. Fiore, "The Dominican Study: Public Library Summer Reading Programs Close the Reading Gap" (River Forest, IL: Graduate School of Library & Information Science, Dominican University, June 2010), 47, https://www.oregon.gov/osl/LD/youthsvcs/srp.certificates/dominicanstudy.pdf.

4. Scholastic Inc., "Kids & Family Reading Report" (6th ed., 2017), 64, www.scholastic.com/readingreport/files/Scholastic-KFRR-6ed-2017.pdf.

5. Ibid., 65.

6. Summer reading participation data were submitted by library staff in 169 of California's 184 library jurisdictions.

7. Scholastic, "Kids," 68.

8. Ibid., 63.

9. Roman et al., "Dominican Study," 55.

10. Beth Yoke, "Adopting a Summer Learning Approach for Increased Impact: A YALSA Position Paper" (Young Adult Library Services Association, April 22, 2016), www.ala .org/yalsa/adopting-summer-learning-approach-increased-impact-yalsa-position-paper.

11. Young Adult Library Services Association, *The Complete Summer Reading Program Manual: From Planning to Evaluation* (Chicago: Young Adult Library Services Association, 2012).

Getting It Right
Quality Principles and Indicators

AFTER SEVERAL YEARS OF EXPERIENCE DEVELOP-
ing and implementing the new outcome measures and
an emphasis on outreach, the advising librarians who
have participated in our action research groups saw the
need to expand our original vision by articulating the
principles that contribute to quality summer programs
implemented according to this model. The result was a
set of four quality principles, each with a series of indicators that would enable
a library to know if that principle was met.[1]

The quality principles and indicators were designed to be used in combination to help library staff develop, maintain, and demonstrate the quality of
their programs, achieve the statewide summer outcomes, reach out effectively
to the community, and communicate with stakeholders. They were developed
in consultation with the California library community over a period of eighteen
months and were completed in 2015. They highlight the four key strengths of
summer programming as identified by California library staff and illustrate and
represent the transformation of California's summer programs. Notably, while
the principles and indicators were designed to guide and reflect our twenty-
first-century public library programming, they also echo some of the founding
principles of the program that were described in chapter 1: for example, programs should be designed to motivate children to keep reading in the summer,

all reading is good reading, programs should be taken out into the community, and summer should have "a freshness of approach" that is different from methods which are followed by teachers during the rest of the year.

California's Summer Program Quality Principles and Indicators

1. Summer @ Your Library builds strong communities. Quality indicators:
   a. The program offers opportunities for community members to get involved in activities that benefit the community.
   b. The staff engage community partners to enrich program offerings and increase the visibility, credibility, and reach of the library's efforts.
   c. The staff offer elements of the program in locations beyond the walls of the library in order to reach as many people as possible.
   d. All staff contribute to the program.

2. Summer @ Your Library provides opportunities for learning. Quality indicators:
   a. The program includes a variety of activities that engage people who have different learning styles and interests.
   b. Activities are designed with specific learning objectives in mind.
   c. The program offers learning opportunities that are fun, inspirational, and informational.
   d. The program encourages self-directed learning, discovery, and creativity.

3. Summer @ Your Library celebrates reading and literacy. Quality indicators:
   a. The library advocates that all reading is good reading.
   b. The library enables people to set and meet individual reading and literacy goals.
   c. The library connects people with a rich and diverse collection of reading materials in a variety of formats.
   d. The library offers activities that extend the reading experience.

4. Summer @ Your Library is designed to reach and engage everyone. Quality indicators:

a. The program has something for all ages and all demographic groups in the community.
b. The program is responsive to the cultures, languages, abilities, and other diversities in the community.
c. The staff makes a special effort to reach people who have not previously taken part in the summer program.

These principles and indicators are intended to be used in a variety of ways.

By providing a framework for reflective practice, the principles and indicators can help libraries improve and develop their programs through a self-directed process. They can be used to help staff review their programs; identify assets, opportunities, needs, and challenges; and go on to develop and improve program quality. The principles can be set as program goals, and the indicators can serve as a road map to help libraries achieve those goals.

The principles and indicators provide an impetus for library staff to develop programs that foster community, connections, and enjoyment, and provide value to participants. By creating programs that are designed to build strong communities, provide opportunities for learning, celebrate reading and literacy, and reach and engage everyone, and by focusing program design on activities that meet the indicators, libraries are well-positioned to achieve the statewide outcomes and reach out effectively to underserved groups.

The principles and indicators provide a context and language for communicating to the community, elected officials, funders, partners, and other stakeholders about the value and impact of the library's summer programs, the goals the library has for its program, and the strategies it has identified for achieving those goals. Libraries can use the language in the principles and indicators to let their stakeholders know where they want the summer program to go and what help and support they need to get there.

Finally, the principles and indicators provide libraries and the Summer @ Your Library project with a means of taking a snapshot of the state of summer programming in California—in individual libraries and in cities, counties, regions, and statewide. In 2016, the Summer @ Your Library project began asking library staff to report annually on the extent to which each indicator was present in their summer programs. The information that was gathered illustrated areas of strength and areas where development is needed. It will inform program and training development and will serve as benchmark data for improving on each year.

Starting in 2017, the Summer @ Your Library project implemented a series of training workshops and community conversations to help libraries integrate the principles and indicators into their program planning, facilitate reflective practice, encourage staff to work collaboratively using the framework, and continue to effect positive change in their summer programs.

Los Angeles Public Library: An Early Adopter

The Los Angeles Public Library is an early adopter of the quality principles and indicators. The library used them to guide program planning and to help its summer programs achieve program outcomes in 2017. The library's systemwide use of the framework in summer program planning provides an early model for how the principles and indicators might be used in other libraries.

CASE STUDY

Los Angeles Public Library

In 2017, the Los Angeles Public Library used the quality principles for the first time as a template to plan the summer reading program. In this first year, the library introduced the principles to children's, young adult, and adult librarians as a checklist of sorts to make sure the outreach and programming at each library is as robust and inclusive as possible.

This introduction to the quality principles was something of a soft launch, with a brief description of the principles during the summer kickoff meeting for each level of librarians and then more in-depth discussion during meetings with the advisory board of "librarian IIIs" (subject specialists who have all the responsibilities of a regular librarian but who also do specialized tasks such as running meetings and conducting training) for each level. The librarian IIIs were then expected to discuss the quality principles in more depth at their regional meetings of children's, young adult, and adult librarians.

At the end of summer, librarians were asked to fill out a short survey about how their summer reading programs incorporated the quality principles; from this, the library gleaned some great ideas, pinpointed areas that need more attention, and also assessed how to improve its summer program in 2018.

For the 2018 summer reading program, the LAPL plans to incorporate the quality principles into every stage of the planning process, starting in October 2017, when the committee first meets to create the framework of the program. By building the principles into the summer reading program from the beginning, the library plans to ensure that it is hitting the mark on all the aspects that make a truly impactful summer for the entire community—but they're betting that they will also find it almost magically easy to achieve the summer outcomes for kids, teens, and adults. Win!

The case studies below show how libraries are already achieving many of California's summer quality principles and indicators. Many of the stories illustrate more than one principle, illustrating the holistic nature of the framework and the breadth of impact of California's summer programs.

QUALITY PRINCIPLE 1:
Summer @ Your Library Builds Strong Communities

CASE STUDY

Spanish Club at San Diego County Library

San Diego County Library's Poway Library is located next to the Valley Elementary School, a Spanish-language immersion elementary school. The Poway Library initiated a summer club to help students continue to practice Spanish-speaking skills while school is out. The Spanish club meets every Wednesday during summer break and is open to all elementary school-aged children. Children practice their vocabulary through mini-lessons in Spanish and English. Bilingual teen volunteers from the local high school help to run the program. They play an essential role in helping to translate lessons, teaching vocabulary words, and facilitating breakout group sessions. In return, they gain volunteer hours to fulfill high school requirements and burnish their college applications.

Laura Gonzalez Garcia, parent liaison for Valley Elementary, describes the benefits to the participating children:

> "The Spanish club offers the opportunity for our students in the Dual Language who are learning Spanish to practice their language skills during the summer in a fun, safe environment. For our students who are learning English and are Spanish speakers, the Club en Español gives them the opportunity to be the language model for the non-Spanish-speaking children and this helps boost their confidence, as they don't get the oppotunity often to feel like a leader."

Parents and teachers have also expressed their appreciation for the Spanish club program. A parent of first and third-grade participants said:

> "Please continue offering the Spanish club during the summer. My children love to practice their Spanish (at home we do not speak Spanish) and the teenagers make it so fun. We have been coming to the Library for three years and without something to keep their brains working over the summer I do not know how they can practice their Spanish."

The library has recently modified the curriculum for the Spanish club to revolve around STEAM, and every Spanish club program is now geared toward either science, technology, engineering, art and design, or math. This change aligned the program more closely with the goals and focus of the Valley Elementary School. The program has been vital in demonstrating the library's support for its community of educators and learners, and it has met with praise and positive feedback from both kids and parents. The teen volunteers also loved the change because they got to do more hands-on experiments and were able to teach fun concepts and projects in Spanish, expanding their own vocabulary with more technical language.

The Poway Library's Spanish club has had a positive impact on the community because it demonstrates that the library is supporting teachers and cares about supporting children's education during the summer break.

BUILDS STRONG COMMUNITIES

"The Teen Summer Reading Program is an awesome program which encourages teens to read and develop a skill set to help us later in life. The program has helped me to develop inroads in the library and participate in the local community with Tech Help."

CASE STUDY

Summer Stride at San Francisco Public Library

The San Francisco Public Library's three-month citywide Summer Stride program encourages students and patrons of all ages to track their reading time and to stop by their neighborhood library for books, comics, e-books, audiobooks, and more. In 2016, Summer Stride offered more than 800 learning and exploration programs designed to strengthen literacy skills, build STEM skills, and expand the notion of learning to include active exploration outside of library walls. Although the program focuses on youth, it engages the entire family and adult patrons.

A new partnership with the National Park Service has enhanced STEM-based programs at the library. In 2016, ranger talks took place at the main San Francisco Public Library and its twenty-seven branches, and patrons joined park rangers on free shuttles from nine neighborhood branch libraries to local national parks. Park Book Nooks distributed free books through little free libraries at the parks. And seven branch libraries had "trailheads" installed that offered maps, reading, and resources for visiting national parks in the area. In the words of Christine Lehnerts, superintendent of the Golden Gate National Recreation Area:

> "This partnership with the San Francisco Public Library is a fantastic way for kids and their families to get to know the national parks in their backyard."

The library also offered edible excursions to the San Francisco Ferry Building, presented nine terrarium-building classes, and took its mobile kitchen, Biblio Bistro, to local farmers' markets. A partnership with Chronicle Books, a San Francisco-based publisher of books for adults and children, provides the Summer Stride promotional artwork which, in 2016, highlighted the diversity of the city's communities and the wide range of Summer Stride activities.

The citywide exploration-focused activities have been a huge success. In 2016, 18,644 people participated in the program, 8,310 people read a total of 138,583 hours, and 822 teens volunteered a total of 8,805 hours—27 percent more participants, 69 percent more reading, and 80 percent more teen volunteers than in the previous year.

CASE STUDY

Sacramento Public Library

The Sacramento Public Library has expanded its summer program throughout the county by offering programs in collaboration with community partners. Many school-age children are unable to access transportation to their local library during the summer, so youth services librarians conduct hundreds of outreach visits to community partner sites to bring summer reading to those children.

The library created a group participation game sheet which enables children and teens to take part in summer reading at their summer school, camp, or other program outside of the library building. Librarians visit the mayor's summer reading camp, camps provided by the local food bank and family services, and school district programs, including Summer Matters, SummerQuest, and Kindergarten Readiness Camps. In 2016 library staff reached 6,000 children through outreach efforts alone.

During outreach visits, librarians engage students with the reading program, introduce them to new books and stories, present activities, and distribute books to children who complete the program—enabling those students to add to the number of books in their homes and further helping them to maintain their reading skills during the summer. These comprehensive outreach efforts by the library help partnering community groups provide students with summer learning experiences, raise the library's profile, and strengthen the summer learning community in Sacramento.

QUALITY PRINCIPLE 2: Summer @ Your Library Provides Opportunities for Learning

CASE STUDY

All-Star Readers at San Diego County Library

The All-Star Readers program at San Diego County Library's Lemon Grove Branch provides support and learning opportunities for students who are struggling the most with reading comprehension. It was developed to address a need in the community for affordable summer literacy tutoring for kindergarten students who are just starting to grasp phonics and letter blends.

The program is run mostly by volunteers. It is structured to allow children to visit four literacy stations over the course of one hour, once a week, for eight weeks, and to read with a tutor for fifteen minutes each time. The stations include LEGO® word building, word families, blends, and writing. The stations and the toys make the program fun for both students and volunteers. Every week that the students attend and read ten books they receive a small incentive. At the end of the eight-week session, a celebration is held to honor their hard work.

The library partners with the Lemon Grove School District's kindergarten teachers to reach out intentionally to families that are most in need at the end of the semester, and the curriculum is coordinated with the assistance of a library volunteer who is a retired "reading recovery teacher" from the Lemon Grove School District.

"The reading program keeps me focused over the summer and expands my vocabulary."

"I discovered new books at the library, also new ideas to create my own comic books."

"I discovered new books and how fun it was to participate as a volunteer for the summer library reading challenge."

"I love the summer reading program because when I'm in school I am way too busy to read. With the summer reading program I can read without missing out all my homework."

By occupying a central position between the school district and community families during summer months, the library has helped to bridge the gap in summer learning for at-risk students. It has aligned the library's mission of serving informed, literate, and engaged communities with the school district's established student achievement goals. All-Star Readers has enhanced trust in the library, designating the Lemon Grove Library as a center for literacy in the neighborhood. It has also led to the development of two other summer learning programs that focus on supporting literacy: Wee Readers, a program that places volunteers with struggling readers for twenty-minute reading sessions during the summer months, and Kindergarten Gear Up!, a program that prepares parents and students for the academic and social rigors of kindergarten.

CASE STUDY

Summer Learning and Enrichment Camps at San Mateo County Libraries

Since 2014 the San Mateo County Libraries have provided enrolled summer-learning camps at school sites and libraries and rapidly expanded a new approach to its summer programming. Half of third-graders in this affluent county are not proficient readers, and those disproportionately affected are socioeconomically disadvantaged and of color.

The library designed its evidence-based model to address that achievement gap and to offer the types of high-quality enrichments that provide much of the basis for differences in learning opportunities for children over the summer. The San Mateo County Libraries, with sales tax funding through the county of

San Mateo, began offering their annual summer learning camp in 2014. The summer camps are rooted in the understanding that creativity is a foundational twenty-first-century skill and that by embedding literacy experiences in dynamic projects, all learners can be engaged, supported, and successful—no drilling or work sheets needed.

In 2015, summer learning enrichment camps in San Mateo County operated for five days per week, for eight weeks, for at least four hours per day, offering a minimum of 160 hours of summer programming—as indicated by research and best practices to successfully arrest the summer slide. Seven camps served 185 incoming second- and third-graders identified as struggling readers and from economically disadvantaged families, and the camps provided them with free, high-quality enrichment opportunities that foster a love of reading; hands-on activities in a variety of subjects, largely based on books and reading; daily healthy meals; books to add to their home libraries; field trips; and family literacy nights to celebrate student work and engage parents in their children's literacy development.

The library developed its own original curriculum—designed to align with the Common Core and to meet all state standards for quality summer developmental programs—in partnership with the Center for Childhood Creativity, a research center that aims to bridge the gap between academic research in the fields of neuroscience, education, psychology, and creativity studies, and Headstand.org, a nonprofit that works to combat toxic stress in disadvantaged K-12 students through mindfulness, yoga, and character education.

In 2016, resulting from the positive impacts of the two previous years,[2] the library joined with additional partners to power the Big Lift Inspiring Summers (BLIS) program, which is part of the Big Lift, a countywide collective impact effort that aims to transform early learning in San Mateo County. The library's program expanded to serve 742 kindergarteners and first-graders at school sites in four local school districts, while continuing to serve an additional 84 children at four library camp locations. The BLIS partnership at the school sites allowed for a five-week, full-day program in partnership with the Silicon Valley Community Foundation, the San Mateo County Office of Education, San Mateo County, and BELL (Building Educated Leaders for Life), a national summer learning nonprofit. Library staff served as site coaches and oversaw the work of library interns who led hands-on learning activities, yoga, field trips, healthy meals, and family events. College-aged interns working with the program benefited from comprehensive training and reported an increased likelihood of going into education or public service as a result of the program.

Three additional districts were added as Big Lift communities for 2017. The program expanded to include second graders and served 1,297 children at eleven school sites. As a result of this scale-up, San Mateo County Libraries moved away from library-based programs to better focus on project-based twenty-first-century learning in library-led camps throughout the county, more effectively meeting the need where it exists. Staff from South San Francisco Public Library and Redwood City Public Library also worked as coaches at the camps in their communities. San Mateo County Libraries' summer camps have successfully increased the number of vulnerable youth engaged in summertime learning experiences. Additionally, the program has strengthened relationships between school and library staff, allowing for more effective partnerships and better support for children all year long .

QUALITY PRINCIPLE 3:
Summer @ Your Library Celebrates Reading and Literacy

CASE STUDY

Book Café for Teens at Burbank Public Library

Burbank Public Library's Book Café developed as a way to bring books and reading to teens who are not members of one of the library's three teen book clubs, and provide a venue for teens to relax and talk about their reading during the summer. Starting in 2015, teen librarians created a café-like atmosphere in the library auditorium by covering round tables with butcher paper and providing colored pencils and crayons for teens to write and draw with while they sat, chatted, and enjoyed coffeehouse treats such as cookies and cappuccino. Initially, teens were invited to bring along the books they were reading, sit with people who enjoyed similar types of reading (e.g., fantasy, science fiction, mystery, or realistic fiction) and discuss their books together. However, Book Café has quickly evolved into something more like an Open Mic Night, but with books. Teens stand in front of the room, book-talk their books, and receive respectful attention followed by applause from other teens.

The Book Café program also sometimes includes authors as guests, providing a relaxed environment where authors can interact with teens in an informal and personal way. Sometimes the author's books are offered for sale, but Book Café is more about an in-depth experience with the author than a typical author "event." Teens who attend three of the four Book Café sessions that are offered during the summer may choose a book to keep from a large cart of teen and teen-appeal books that the library purchases for this purpose. The program

"Also, I've gotten back into the habit of reading and love it now."

"My son is a new reader. It helped spark his interest even more and helped develop his reading skills."

"I like best that we had fun reading, playing, and getting fun education. I never loved a library in life. Now I change."

"I believe the summer reading program is a great way of getting others to be hooked on books and exploring activities they usually don't try."

"The reading challenge reminds me to read something during the summer, as the school library was my main source of books to read during the school year."

"Loved it! I love reading in the library because I love stories a lot! So I'm gonna just keep reading for the rest of my life!"

incentivizes free voluntary reading, teaches teens how to share their positive reading experiences with one another, fosters community and connection, and helps teens gain more exposure to books they might enjoy. Book Café is now the most popular Burbank Public Library program with local teens!

CASE STUDY

Summer Reading Club at the Whittier Public Library

The Whittier Public Library's summer reading club for children goes back to 1949. Since the beginning, the club has asked children to give one-on-one oral book reports to staff members or "volunteens" (tweens and teens in eighth grade or above who volunteer to listen to the book reports). This feature brings children and tweens to the library and connects them with staff and teens in the community.

Children up to fourth grade give oral reports on six books over a seven-week period and play an original reading game that typically involves solving riddles and puzzles. Fifth- to eighth-graders give an oral report on four books and take part in a Game of Chance—a Monopoly-like game that helps them choose the books they will read. After eighth grade, children and tweens can transition to the teen and then the adult program, which helps ensure that summer reading is a program for the whole family.

The programs culminate in a large carnival-like community party at a local park. Parents and teachers say that the oral book reports have helped their children combat the summer slide. Many of the summer "volunteers" have become library employees over the years.

The library offers many other reading opportunities during the summer. Parents, grandparents, and other caregivers read sixteen books to early learners in the Read-To-Me Club, and at the end they receive a certificate and a party. The Summer Reading Club On-The-Go enables day carers, preschoolers, and adults with special needs to take part in summer reading off-site and visit the library to check out books. In 2017, the library launched a Pop-Up Mobile Library and took summer reading on the road. The staff takes great pride in the long history and tradition of the Whittier Public Library's Summer Reading Club, its strong focus on reading, and how it helps foster a love of reading among the families of Whittier.

QUALITY PRINCIPLE 4: Summer @ Your Library is Designed to Reach and Engage Everyone

CASE STUDY

Contra Costa County Library's Pleasant Hill Library: Programming for the Whole Family

The Contra Costa County Library's Pleasant Hill Library has asked: how can we expand our summertime offerings from ages zero to 100 and span the generations? It believes that libraries have many opportunities to increase accessibility to family members, and it's easy to engage more members of the community when everyone is invited. The Pleasant Hill Library is using the following strategies to encourage multi-generational participation:

- Make things musical! Music can bring everyone together, get them moving, and invite the community into undiscovered cultures. The library is going beyond age-specific restrictions in storytimes and is using music to bridge the age gaps. Music is magic.
- Design maker and craft events with the youngest in mind. Hands-on science activities like slime and bread making are fun for all ages but have a strong sensory appeal to the early learners. For artistic creations, the library offers a variety of materials for a variety of ages and skills: stickers and stampers are easier to wield than other implements. When library staff cover the tables with butcher paper for messy events, they leave out crayons for little hands. Why not?

- Add DUPLO® and Mindstorms robotics to open up the LEGO® Club to babies and brainiacs alike.
- Enhance the permanent spaces with colorful carpets, toys, and furnishings to excite early learners while allowing big brother or sister to get the most out of higher-level programs. This means the whole family can remain engaged and extend their stay.

CASE STUDY

Inclusive Summer Reading Programs at Corona Public Library

Inclusivity is a priority for the Corona Public Library, and this priority is now reflected in the summer reading program. The library has traditionally offered a variety of summer programs based on participants' ages and grade levels, including programs for babies, toddlers, preschoolers, young readers, school-aged children, tweens, teens, and adults. In 2016, it introduced an Adaptive summer program for teens and adults with special needs and an Adult Reading Assistance summer program for tutor/learner pairs in the library's adult literacy program. Both programs promote participation regardless of reading ability.

The Adaptive summer reading program included weekly sensory storytimes comprising theme-based stories, crafts, and activities. Participants could spin for prizes and were given books to take home at every storytime. They were encouraged to attend at least five storytimes to complete the summer reading program, although reading for an hour on their own could substitute for attending a session. Several locally based group homes and day programs participated, and the program was so successful that the library has added monthly sensory storytimes to its year-round library programming.

The Library and Recreation Services Department is becoming known in Corona as a place for fun and interesting programming for teens and adults with special needs. Using The Harwood Institute's Turning Outward methods and practices, the department has held community conversations and developed strong partnerships in order to gather information about community aspirations. That information is now informing the library's Adaptive summer reading program and other events for community members with special needs.

In the Adult Reading Assistance summer program, tutor/learner pairs were encouraged to participate in the summer program as a team. Reading together for an hour earned them one spinning wheel prize. After five sessions, the pairs were entered into the Player Seven grand prize drawing for a basket promoting the love of reading. The library also hosted Adult Reading Assistance workshops on personal growth and self-esteem and celebrated at the end of the program with an Adult Reading Assistance potluck.

The Adult Reading Assistance summer program promoted the literacy program, motivated participants already enrolled in summer activities, and solidified the tutor/learner pairs as a team. The 2017 program included more literacy-based workshops, incorporated California's Library Literacy Roles and Goals evaluation tools more closely, and increased participants' confidence in reading and writing. The 2017 Adaptive and Adult Reading Assistance summer reading programs showed the highest percentage of finishers among all the offered "Designer Groups."

To help promote the various summer reading "Designer Groups," the library has also added a citywide staff element with a special grand prize drawing for city of Corona staff. The library aims to make reading and the love of reading a priority for the community, and buy-in by city of Corona staff will be another means of achieving that goal.

DESIGNED TO REACH AND ENGAGE EVERYONE

"I like sharing the experience with my kids. They see my commitment to reading, we have fun racing to see who can reach the goal first, and have fun going to choose our book prizes. It is a family affair!"

"I loved taking my son and younger daughter to the summer activities. I wish we had been able to attend all of them because they are great!"

"I haven't really read since I graduated college and this got me going again."

CASE STUDY

Sacramento Public Library

The Sacramento Public Library's summer reading program is designed to engage people of all ages and families as well as individuals. This approach is critical to engaging the entire Sacramento community with its public libraries, and it has resulted in an increase in program participation over the past four years.

A consistent message and a streamlined goal and program structure for all ages have been key to the library's success: "read five books and win a prize" is a message that is easy for staff and volunteers to convey and easy for the community to understand. Staff training ensures that the program is consistent in all twenty-eight library locations, and all public-facing staff are expected to attend training (or view an online training) on talking points and best practices.

Summer reading for pre-readers is based on the five practices that caregivers engage in with their child to prepare them to be ready to read—talking, singing, reading, writing, and playing. Rewarding caregivers for these activities with a book for their child affirms what they are already doing and provides ideas for continuing to support their child's development. Offering summer reading for pre-readers also strengthens the library's partnerships with Birth and Beyond centers, kindergarten readiness camps, and Head Starts in supporting early literacy practices within families. And the pre-reader program provides a hook to get parents to participate as well!

The program for school-age children includes a range and variety of activity options to ensure that it is accessible to students from a wide variety of backgrounds. In addition, students read and log books of their choosing, ensuring that the program is a celebration of reading, free from judgment about reading level, and is inclusive of children with learning disabilities and those building their reading fluency and competence.

The teen summer reading program provides opportunities for youth to serve as volunteers and interns supporting outreach and programming. Teens are coordinators for the library's summer lunch program, serving peers and younger children in their community. In addition, the library system's Teen Advisory Board plans and leads a large summer evening event for teens held at three regionally accessible branches.

The adult program enables entire families to participate together, encouraging caregivers and other adults to model positive reading behaviors. It has also helped the library and its community partners to engage adults with developmental disabilities, a group that is often underserved. Moreover, the adult program also allows the library to engage some of its most enthusiastic supporters—including the Friends of the Library, loyal library visitors, and board members—in its biggest program of the year, summer reading.

In fall 2016, in the first Summer @ Your Library survey asking the library community to report on the extent to which the indicators are present in their summer programs, librarians responded positively to the principles and indicators. Feedback included:

"Keep up the good work! They are challenging and when used will strengthen the results of SRP in the community."

"It's helpful to see areas we can grow in. Thank you for providing a framework to inform proposed changes in our Summer Program. Through evaluating our program this way, we better prepare ourselves to demonstrate the Library's value as an educational institution."

"These quality principles and indicators are a good yardstick for us to measure the effectiveness of our summer program and, when used in our planning process, can increase its effectiveness."

The principles give staff new ways to talk about summer at their libraries. The four principles demonstrate the value of this seasonal initiative, and the indicators offer concrete advice about how to achieve those principles. Together, they are creating a new shared vocabulary about the library's role in summer reading, summer learning, and community-building—something that has been critical in establishing partnerships with other agencies and in helping libraries engage in collective impact efforts such as the Summer Matters campaign that is discussed in the following chapter.

Notes

1. California's public library summer program quality principles and indicators were developed with support from ScholarShare/TIAA-CREF.

2. One hundred percent of the ninety-nine children who completed pre- and post-camp assessment surveys increased or retained their existing literacy skills, and 43 percent improved their instructional reading level. Eighty-eight percent of youth stated they felt better about themselves as readers and learners after participating in the library camp.

CHAPTER 7

Summer Matters
We are Stronger and More
Effective Together

N RECENT YEARS, LIBRARIANS, EDUCATORS, POLICY MAK-
ers, families, and other stakeholders have become increasingly
aware of the long-lasting effects of summer learning loss on children and teens. A child's need for meaningful learning and enrichment does not end in June when school doors close for summer
vacation. All children need to be engaged, actively learning, physically active, and eating a balanced diet during summer. Research
has shown that without ongoing summer opportunities to reinforce and learn
skills, children (and especially those in low-income communities) fall behind
dramatically in many areas of academic achievement and risk negative health
impacts. Low-income children are nearly three grades behind their more affluent peers in reading by the end of fifth grade as a result of summer learning
loss.[1] Furthermore, unequal summer learning opportunities during the elementary school years are responsible for two-thirds of the ninth-grade achievement gap between lower and higher-income youth, and as a result, low-income
youth are less likely to graduate from high school or enter college.[2]

These data—plus work carried out by the National Summer Learning Association, among others, to raise awareness of the negative outcomes associated
with summer learning loss—have provided an impetus for the development and
acceleration of efforts, large and small, across the United States to provide children and teens with access to summer learning and enrichment opportunities.

In this chapter, we provide details about one initiative in California that facilitated productive partnership and outreach opportunities for libraries engaged in summer learning programs for young people. We hope that our experiences will provide a model for other collaborative efforts addressing summer learning loss, and for libraries elsewhere to engage in citywide, county, regional, and statewide collective impact efforts.

The Summer Matters Campaign

In California, the Summer Matters campaign, a statewide network of school districts, county offices of education, program providers, advocacy organizations, state and city public agencies, legislators, and funders, is working collaboratively to expand and improve access to high-quality summer learning opportunities for California students. The vision of Summer Matters is that all young people in California have equitable access to high-quality summer learning opportunities to support their year-round learning and well-being. The campaign was launched in 2008 with funding from the David and Lucile Packard Foundation. It is a collaborative effort, coordinated by the Partnership for Children and Youth, a nonprofit intermediary focused on after-school, summer, and community school practice and policy.[3]

By providing summer programs for all ages, free of charge, in a trusted space, libraries make a significant contribution to community-based efforts to provide all children and teens with access to summer learning and enrichment activities. As part of the Summer Matters campaign, California's public libraries have contributed to a coordinated statewide effort to address summer learning loss and, in doing so, have extended the impact of their summer programs and reached previously underserved community members.

The Summer Matters campaign has implemented an intensive, multifaceted approach to expand and improve summer learning in California. This work includes supporting model program practices, developing standards and tools for quality improvement, promoting summer learning to education leaders and state-level decision-makers, and sponsoring legislation to improve funding for summer programming.

Since 2008, the campaign has successfully

- created twelve high-quality summer learning programs that showcase best practices and support year-round learning and well-being;
- developed and promoted the use of quality standards and a quality

improvement system that reached over 1,000 program providers in 2016;

- generated momentum and support for summer learning among California's education, elected, business, civic, and philanthropic leaders, including a statewide work group on summer learning at the California Department of Education and over 150 school leaders signed on as Summer Matters champions;
- engaged 143 organizations in supporting summer learning through the Summer Matters Roundtable;
- raised awareness about the devastating effects of summer learning loss and the need for high-quality opportunities during summer for all youth through stories in large and small media markets across California;
- fostered the development of state, regional, and local networks of organizations, including libraries, that are working and learning together to address summer learning loss;
- increased summer programs' access to technical assistance providers in southern California, the northern part of the state, the San Francisco Bay Area, and the Central Valley that are working and learning together to address summer learning loss;
- passed four pieces of state legislation to increase awareness and access to summer learning; and
- increased the number of youth served by summer learning programs across the state.

The Summer Matters campaign will continue to build statewide momentum and programming across California through a network-building strategy. The network will strengthen connections among the regional and statewide organizations already involved in the campaign and create opportunities for new partners to engage with it.

Summer Matters Library Partnerships

As demonstrated with the network approach, a guiding principle of the Summer Matters campaign is that community collaboration produces effective and sustainable results. From the start, campaign leaders have engaged libraries and other agencies, such as state parks, the PTA, and YMCA, to help community- and school-based summer programs provide rich, integrated, and engaging learning opportunities for children and teens. As a result, many of the summer learning programs that are part of the Summer Matters campaign made library partnerships, visits, and activities an integral part of their summer curricula.

Between 2009 and 2016, these library partnerships were developed with the aid of funds from the David and Lucile Packard Foundation. The foundation's assistance enabled Summer @ Your Library project staff to support the partnerships with programming materials, online resources, and an evaluation framework. Project staff worked with participating librarians and summer program staff to closely document successes and lessons learned and to develop a comprehensive set of resources and case studies to help others learn from their experiences and create meaningful summer partnerships.

Libraries are ideally positioned to contribute to collaborative efforts to address summer learning loss, just as they contribute to other efforts to advance social well-being. The Institute of Museum and Library Services states:

> "There are a variety of ways that museums and libraries already contribute to collective impact across multiple dimensions of social well-being. These include: guiding vision and strategy; supporting aligned activities; establishing shared measurement practices; building public will; advancing policy; mobilizing funding. The intersection of collective impact and social well-being is where museums and libraries can position themselves as catalysts for change."[4]

In addition, by participating in collaborative efforts, libraries gain new partners, supporters, and advocates, extend their reach, and strengthen their community networks. California librarians are also engaged in another collective effort, the Campaign for Grade-Level Reading. They agree that the relationships they have developed and strengthened with local school districts, housing authorities, and nonprofit agencies like the United Way are key benefits resulting from their participation.[5] Summer Matters is yielding similar positive consequences.

Benefits for Libraries, Summer Learning Programs, and Children, Teens, and Their Families

The Summer Matters library partnerships have benefited the libraries and summer learning programs that formed relationships as well as the children, teens, and families they serve. The partnerships have connected libraries with previously underserved families; helped summer learning program staff provide students with a variety of summer enrichment activities; strengthened local summer learning community networks; and introduced children, teens, and their families to the public library and its services.

Children and teens who connected with the library during their Summer Matters summer learning camps reported that they enjoyed visiting the library and taking part in library programs. This is particularly significant because many of the children and teens who attended Summer Matter summer learning programs are not library regulars and had never taken part in a public library's summer reading program before enrolling in a Summer Matters summer learning camp. Data and anecdotal evidence tell us that most children and teens who typically take part in public libraries' summer reading programs already enjoy books, reading, and visiting the library.[6] The Summer Matters partnerships helped libraries connect with students who don't view the library as a destination during the summer or at any other time of the year. The partnerships were an effective way for libraries to reach out and provide services to underserved community members, and library staff appreciated the opportunity to connect with youth they don't usually see during the summer and families they don't already know.

The library partnerships have helped summer program staff meet literacy goals and outcomes, enhance their curricula, offer field trips, and keep students reading during the summer months. Moreover, the partnerships helped program staff develop their good summer learning programs into great summer learning programs. The Partnership for Children and Youth and the Summer Matters campaign have established best practices for summer learning programs. These practices are grounded in research and experimentation that have been conducted during the campaign. They assert that in order to achieve excellence and fulfill their potential, summer learning programs must

STUDENTS

"I enjoy the library's summer reading program because it makes me feel like I am learning more and more." (student)

"I really like the help the library has given me! I have improved my reading." (student)

"I will come back to the library because I like the activities and books." (student)

"I feel like everyone should go to the library." (student)

1. broaden youth horizons,
2. include a wide range of activities,
3. help youth build mastery,
4. foster cooperative learning,
5. promote healthy habits, and
6. last for at least one month.

Libraries are ideal partners to help summer programs fulfill these criteria: youths' horizons are broadened when they visit the library for the first time and go on to develop a relationship with their local library; libraries offer a wide range of fun and engaging activities during the summer; library resources can help youth build mastery by working on a task or project and working cooperatively with friends; a library habit is a healthy habit; and summer reading programs are designed to last from the end of one school year to the start of the next.

Partnership Models

"The highlight was the family night that the library offered. Students, parents, and families were grateful to have a night devoted to the summer program. At the event, library employees had a storytelling, a fake campfire (connected to 'our survive and thrive' theme), stories related to our theme, food, and much more." (program staff member, Oakland)

"We conducted numerous visits which included research assistance, readalouds, and summer reading support." (program staff member, San Francisco)

Summer Matters library partnerships were developed in a variety of California public libraries—large and small, city and county, urban, suburban, and rural.[7] Each partnership evolved to meet the needs of the local community, with some libraries hosting only a few meaningful library visits over the course of the summer and others becoming an integral part of their partner's weekly schedule throughout the summer. In each case, the library became part of a coordinated and holistic effort to expose children and teens to a variety of high-quality and engaging summer learning activities, and children and teens were introduced to a community resource that can provide them and their families with programs, support, services, and resources long after summer ends.

The most successful Summer Matters library partnerships benefited from coordinated planning efforts between library staff and summer program staff; were designed to engage children and teens who do not typically visit the library; drew on libraries' strengths; and were manageable for libraries to administer during the busy summer period—helping to ensure that the partnership could be sustained. Typical programming activities included scavenger hunts and library bingo, which introduced youth to library resources; hands-on programs encouraging youth to take part in art-making, crafts, LEGO® building, sports and games, animal experiences, scientific experimentation, video-making, and music-making; read-alouds; film and book discussions; and, of course, the summer reading program—all of which demonstrated the range of activities regularly on offer at the library. Librarians also visited program sites to give book talks, facilitate programming, hand out summer reading prizes, and promote the library.

Although the library partnerships provided children and teens with access to similar library programs and activities, they differed in approach and emphasis because each was tailored to the local community's needs and resources. As a result, the Summer Matters campaign has fostered the development of a number of different partnership models that can be replicated in other communities.

LIBRARIANS

"Partnerships like these benefit the library as the organization brings their students. The organization is trusted by the students and parents . . . The organization validates the importance of the library and its use. That is the most powerful message. We support each other to strengthen the importance of literature to our youth."
(librarian, Oakland)

"For many of the students who were in attendance, July 24, 2013, was the day that they first stepped into their community library. Not only did they come to our site, but many received their first library card."
(librarian, Santa Ana)

"This group of kids became our messengers, to tell about library events, activities, and service updates to people that they know, which helped to promote our service."
(librarian, Los Angeles)

Dovetailing the Library Experience and Summer Program Experience

Librarians at San Francisco Public Library's Portola Library and their partners at the Hillcrest Elementary School worked together closely to develop library experiences that would directly support the curriculum at the school site. When the Hillcrest curriculum focused on the history and culture of the local community, library programming included local history activities, workshops by local artists and musicians, and read-alouds focusing on neighborhood landmarks and the San Francisco Bay. Similarly, librarians at the San Bernardino Public Library hosted book and film discussion programs, author talks, and comic book-writing workshops for students enrolled in the school district's CAPS program, in order to reinforce the critical thinking skills that students were developing at their summer learning program. When librarians and summer program staff work together to coordinate programming, the library partnership helps summer program staff deliver their curriculum and helps librarians demonstrate to students how the library can support their studies and relate to their lives.

Engaging the Whole Family

Family open nights were at the heart of the Summer Matters partnerships developed by the Oakland and Whittier public libraries. In Oakland, library staff worked with the East Bay Asian Youth Center (EBAYC) to bring EBAYC families to the library for evenings of storytelling, crafts, scavenger hunts, and dinner. Similarly, Whittier's popular literacy nights for the families of students enrolled in the Whittier School District's Jump Start pro-

SUMMER LEARNING PROGRAM STAFF

"The partnership was a huge success and added value to our program immensely. Our students were able to visit the library numerous times and hear guest speakers, do research, check out books, and interact with librarians at the branch at the school."
(program staff member, San Francisco)

"Thank you so much for the opportunity to connect our schools with your libraries in a meaningful way."
(program staff member, Los Angeles)

"I noticed the student reading increase throughout the summer session."
(program staff member, Los Angeles)

gram included crafts, musical performances, stories, and ice cream, and they attracted students, their parents, and siblings of all ages. Engaging the whole family can be key to encouraging children to be regular library users, and evening events, held in conjunction with other daytime activities for students, can provide library staff with opportunities to engage and focus on previously underserved families in a relaxed and informal setting.

Bringing Youth to the Library

Librarians at the Santa Ana Public Library and their partners at the THINK Together program focused on providing students with opportunities to visit and experience the library during the summer. Most of the children and teens attending THINK Together had difficulty visiting the library during the school year: many live too far from the library to visit on foot, and their parents are unable to transport them. Bringing students through the library doors, introducing them to the space, and providing them with a positive library experience—which included providing students with books they could take home and keep—was a priority in Santa Ana. Many children in low-income families face challenges that are similar to those in Santa Ana, and library partnerships that bring kids across the library threshold and directly engage them with the space can play an invaluable role in raising awareness of the library and sparking an interest in future visits to it.

"Having the library be part of the summer program provided books to kids who don't have them at home, an opportunity to read and help either maintain or increase their reading levels over the summer, and kids got excited about reading because they got their own library card, which was huge and special for many of them." (program staff member, Gilroy)

"Some of the students had not been to the library before and now see the value in it and really enjoyed the experience. The enthusiasm and energy of local librarians really won them over!" (program staff member, Glenn County)

Taking the Library to the Youth

Librarians from the Los Angeles Public Library provided their partners at the LA's BEST program with summer reading group outreach kits, including reading logs and activities, which they supplemented with visits to the summer learning program sites. The kits enable students to participate in the summer reading program at their school sites, and help program staff engage students with summer reading while tracking students' progress toward their reading goals. During outreach visits, librarians gave book talks and promoted library programs. When libraries do not have the resources to invite large groups to the library, outreach kits and visits can help library staff engage children and teens with library resources, help program staff facilitate students' participation in summer reading, and provide students with the opportunities to see librarians out in the community.

A Focus on Reading

The Gilroy Public Library, part of the Santa Clara County Library District, focused on developing a reading culture among students from the Gilroy Unified School District's Power School. Students visited the library weekly, for a full day, during which library staff walked them through the process of participating in the summer reading program; guided their reading choices; engaged them in craft activities, film screenings, and book talks; and provided them with free reading time. To extend the benefits of this partnership beyond summer, the library and the Power School began collaborating year-round to extend the summer experience. At the Orland and Willows libraries in Glenn County, there was a similar focus on summer reading for students enrolled in the Glenn County Office of Education's summer programs, but on a schedule and scale to fit those libraries' limited staffing. Students walked over for hour-long visits to the library, where they received introductions to the summer reading program and heard about upcoming events that they and their families could enjoy at the library. They sat for a read-aloud, received an introduction to the services available to them at the library, and selected books to take home and keep.

Library Orientations for Summer Program Staff

Library orientations for staff were an important part of many of the Summer Matters library partnerships. Program staff are typically trusted by students and their parents, and they can play an important role in encouraging families to trust and value the library. It was therefore important that program staff were engaged with library programming and were well-informed about library services so they could endorse the library to their students and help them make positive connections with library staff.

Partnership Readiness

Successful collaborations and partnerships typically develop slowly, and it is not unusual for partners to need to address challenges and obstacles before achieving a meaningful and sustainable relationship. The Summer Matters library partnerships were no exception. Although library staff and summer program staff were working toward the same goal of providing enriching summer learning opportunities for children and teens, their organizations had quite different organizational cultures and different methods of achieving their goals, which often made it difficult for staff to partner effectively at the start. Drawing on this experience, Summer @ Your Library project staff worked with library staff and summer learning program staff to develop a set of resources to help others establish partnerships, navigate challenges, and ultimately develop meaningful and sustainable relationships.

The partnership readiness tool created by the project can help agencies establish whether a potential partnership is right for them and right for them right now. Partnership readiness and effectiveness can be evaluated using several key criteria:

- A personal/professional connection between at least one staff person in each partnering organization and a clear communication channel (if necessary, a single point of contact)
- An understanding and respect for one another's organizational culture, practices, procedures, capacity, and intentions and goals for the partnership
- Staff members who see value in the partnership
- Staff members who are outreach- and partnership-minded and know that pursuing a successful partnership can require tenacity, enthusiasm, and dedication to that partnership
- Staff members with strong planning and communication skills
- Adequate staffing levels
- Potential for longevity (many partnerships improve over time as staff members become increasingly familiar with one another, and one another's organizations)

The more of these criteria that are present, the more likely it is that the partnership will be a success. We recommend that partners recognize and acknowledge missing criteria, because each will require accommodation in making the partnership ultimately successful.

Other resources we created include tips on partnering effectively; information that library staff wanted summer program staff to know about libraries, and information that summer program staff wanted library staff to know about their community- and school-based summer learning programs; and programming suggestions tailored specifically to library partnerships that are designed to introduce large groups of children and teens to the library during the busy summer period—all of which can be found at www.calchallenge.org. We invite others to use the resources to create successful, meaningful partnerships between public libraries and school- and community-based summer learning programs.

Create a Summer Learning Partnership!

Based on the successes we have seen in the Summer Matters campaign communities, we encourage libraries and summer learning programs to reach out to one another and make the library an integral and intentional part of community- and school-based summer programs. And we encourage library administrators to support staff in forming strategic partnerships with summer learning programs and with city, county, regional, or state summer learning initiatives, to strengthen the library's impact and standing in the community, and to help keep kids reading and learning all summer long.

A first step for libraries is reaching out to the local school district to find out what kind of summer programs they have and who the coordinator is. While it can be hard to find out this basic information in a large school district, some possible first points of contact include the after-school or expanded learning programs office or the student support services office. Often summer activities are housed there. Once the right person has been identified, it's a matter of assessing the criteria listed above and taking the first steps to defining your vision and activities for a great summer partnership.

Notes

1. National Summer Learning Association, "Smarter Summers. Brighter Futures," www.summerlearning.org.

2. Karl L. Alexander, Doris R. Entwisle, and Linda Steffel Olson, "Lasting Consequences of the Summer Learning Gap," *American Sociological Review* 72, no. 2 (April 2007): 167–80.

3. Summer Matters, "Doesn't Every Child Deserve an Enriching, Memorable Summer?" www.summermatters.net.

4. Michael H. Norton and Emily Dowdall, "Strengthening Networks, Sparking Change: Museums and Libraries as Community Catalysts" (Reinvestment Fund Policy Solutions, 2016), 11, www.imls.gov/sites/default/files/publications/documents/community -catalyst-report-january-2017.pdf.

5. Interviews between the author and librarians in San Diego, Santa Barbara, Marin County, and Sacramento.

6. Susan Roman, Deborah T. Carran, and Carole D. Fiore, "The Dominican Study: Public Library Summer Reading Programs Close the Reading Gap" (River Forest, IL: Graduate School of Library & Information Science, Dominican University, June 2010), www .oregon.gov/osl/LD/youthsvcs/srp.certificates/dominicanstudy.pdf.

7. Fresno, Gilroy, Glenn County, Los Angeles, Oakland, Sacramento, San Bernardino, San Francisco, San José, Santa Ana, and Whittier.

CHAPTER 8

Lunch at the Library

Coauthored with Patrice Chamberlain

UBLIC LIBRARIES ACROSS CALIFORNIA ARE TRANS-
forming their summers by embracing an unlikely program
as part of their summertime operations—the U.S. Department of Agriculture's (USDA's) summer meal program. By
providing snacks and meals, free of charge, public libraries
are helping to ensure that low-income, food-insecure children and teens have access to healthy food and are engaged
during the summer months so that they are prepared to return to school in the
fall ready to learn.

In California, public libraries' summer meal programs have become very successful very quickly. These programs are introducing families to library resources
and providing families with opportunities for intergenerational experiences
and social interaction. They are helping libraries provide teens with youth development opportunities and workforce readiness skills. They are engaging local
leaders with the library, increasing the visibility of library services, and providing a catalyst for new community partnerships. Moreover, they are helping
libraries achieve California's statewide summer outcomes by fostering commu-

An earlier version of this chapter appeared in Public Libraries *in 2015 under the title
"Nourishing Bodies and Minds When School Is Out: California's Public Library Summer
Meal Programs."*[1]

nity and connections, and value and enjoyment, and being an effective means of engaging new and previously underserved families with the library. Most importantly, of course, they are feeding hungry children and teens.

This chapter provides information about the genesis, operations, and best practices of California's public library summer meal programs as well as the positive outcomes that have been achieved.

The Need for Summer Meal Programs

There is a significant need to increase the number of accessible and appealing summer meal programs in every state. When school lets out for summer vacation, many low-income children lose access to learning and enrichment opportunities and the nutrition provided by school lunch and breakfast programs.

A 2013 nationwide survey of parents found that more than 40 percent of low-income families had a harder time making ends meet in summer than during the school year, with some reporting that they did not have enough food during the summer break.[2] In addition, we know that low-income youth fall further behind in academic skills, particularly reading, during the summer break and experience greater summer learning loss than their higher-income peers, thus widening the achievement gap.[3] Research shows that low-income children are nearly three grades behind their more affluent peers in reading by the end of fifth grade as a cumulative consequence of summer learning loss.[4] Unequal summer learning opportunities during the elementary school years account for about two-thirds of the ninth-grade achievement gap, contributing to a lower likelihood that low-income youth will graduate from high school or enter college in comparison to middle-income students.[5]

In some neighborhoods, the omnipresence of unhealthy food options poses additional challenges for families. Research shows that children gain weight two to three times faster during the summer than during the school year; those already at risk of obesity are at even greater risk for excessive weight gain.[6] To help address summer weight gain, the Society of Behavioral Medicine has recommended the adoption of school district, state, and federal policies that facilitate

> "(1) partnerships between school districts and community organizations to provide affordable summertime programming; (2) strategic efforts by schools and communities to encourage families to enroll in and attend summertime programming . . . ; (3) adoption of joint use/shared use

agreements to promote use of indoor and outdoor school facilities to provide affordable programming during the summer months; and (4) implementation of strategies that help summer programs achieve the Healthy
Eating and Physical Activity (HEPA) standards, which have been endorsed
by the Healthy Out-of-School Time (HOST) coalition."[7]

The impact of inadequate nutrition on students' ability to learn is significant.
Although the relationship between food insecurity and childhood obesity is
complex, both are associated with lower academic gains, increased absenteeism
and tardiness, social and mental health problems, and "poor developmental
trajectories."[8]

Researchers at Washington University have traced the negative impact of
poverty on brain development and highlighted the links between inadequate
nutrition, poor education, and other conditions of stress on developmental
outcomes.[9] Summer can add to those stressful conditions by creating a perfect
storm for risk of food insecurity, obesity, and summer learning loss. Our collective imagination of summertime includes children playing outside and enjoying
summer camps, yet summer can present a very different reality for those living
in neighborhoods with limited access to healthy food options, summer learning
opportunities, and safe places to play.

During the 2014–2015 school year, 21,500,000 students received a subsi-
dized lunch.[10] The Washington, DC-based Food Research and Action Center
(FRAC) reports that

"for every 100 low-income children who ate school lunches during the
2014–2015 school year, just 15.8 children, or roughly one in six, participated in the Summer Nutrition Programs in July 2015."[11]

That is, fewer than one in six children who needed summer meals received them.
In California in 2015, for every 100 children who received free or reduced-price
lunches during the school year, only 19.2 participated in a USDA summer meal
program.[12] The cost of low participation is significant. Across the country, mil-
lions of children and teens do not have regular, nutritious meals or learning
opportunities during the summer.

Some of the most common barriers that prevent families from participating
in USDA summer meal programs are a lack of sites in the community, a lack of
knowledge about summer meal sites, and a lack of sites that appeal to families.
In California, as in many states, communities are still trying to rebound from
the Great Recession that began in 2008, and cuts to summer school and other

summer programs have meant cuts to school-based summer meal programs. Recent cuts left 50 percent fewer school-based summer meal sites between 2009 and 2010, for example.[13] Parents and caregivers are looking for activities to keep children and teens engaged during the summer, as well as nutrition support to help where limited family summer budgets fall short, yet budget cuts have left many school, city, and community-based meal providers with a lack of places to serve meals or a lack of activities and programming at existing sites.

The stark contrast between school year and summer child nutrition program data, and the increasing body of research on summer learning loss, have provided a call to action for many agencies to establish themselves as summer meal sites. In recent years, public libraries have emerged as natural spaces for serving meals to children whose access to healthy food disappears when school ends: these libraries are accessible community spaces at the heart of the neighborhood, often acting as an equalizing force in communities divided by socioeconomic barriers; they are rich with learning activities and opportunities, all free of charge to the user; and library staff share a commitment to serving all members of the community. As the American Library Association states:

> "Public libraries serve as community anchors that address economic, educational, and health disparities in the community."[14]

Moreover, libraries are trusted and valued by the community. The Pew Research Center reports that Americans believe libraries are important assets within their communities and improve the quality of life. Libraries are particularly valued by low-income families and are perceived as providing resources that parents cannot provide for their children at home.[15]

Lunch at the Library

California has proven to be a perfect testing ground for experimenting with public libraries' summer meal programs because of its size, diversity, severe need, and its adventurous librarians who are willing to explore the possibilities. A statewide project called Lunch at the Library helps California's public libraries establish themselves as successful summer meal sites. Project staff help libraries connect with meal sponsors and provide training, support, and resources, including a mentorship program, for library staff. The rapid growth of successful summer meal programs in California is due in large part to Lunch at the Library and to three defining features of the project:

1. *Collaboration:* The project is led jointly by two statewide agencies, the California Library Association, the professional association for the California library community; and the California Summer Meal Coalition, a program of the Institute for Local Government that works to combat food insecurity and childhood obesity by ensuring that low-income children and youth have access to healthy food when school is out, and also builds out-of-school-time collaborations by increasing access to USDA summer meal programs. The two agencies have established a strong working partnership that allows them to bring together the library community and the health and nutrition community, learn from both, leverage resources from both, and provide holistic support to California's public library summer meal programs.

2. *Evaluation:* From the start, Lunch at the Library has emphasized ongoing evaluation and reflection, and it has provided library staff with tools that generate quantitative and qualitative data. Each year, project staff and librarians draw on survey data, feedback from families, and observations from colleagues to develop training and resources that are grounded in the successes and lessons learned at summer meal sites.

3. *Funding:* The Lunch at the Library project was created in 2013 with seed funding from the David and Lucile Packard Foundation, and it receives Library Services and Technology Act funds from the Institute of Museum and Library Services, administered in California by the state librarian. Grant funding has enabled the California Library Association and the California Summer Meal Coalition to assign staff members to Lunch at the Library and take the time needed to develop a rigorous, sustainable, and effective project.

Program Impact in California

Summer meal programs are now signature summer programs for many California libraries. Across the state, staff and volunteers provide meals and snacks in community rooms, teen centers, library stacks, and more while school is out. In 2016 California's public libraries served over 203,000 meals and 60,000 snacks at 139 sites, and the programs have expanded rapidly since the recorded 21,000 meals served at 17 sites in 2013. Of the 5,147 children and caregivers who completed surveys at California's public library summer meal sites in 2016, 19 percent reported that they don't get lunch anywhere else but the library during the summer—illustrating the significant need for these programs.

The Ontario City Library is an example of a library that has fully integrated its summer meal and summer reading programs.

CASE STUDY
Ontario City Library

The Ontario City Library started offering summer meals in 2015. Staff and volunteers witnessed new families coming in for summer lunch, and then they witnessed those same families staying in the building and making use of all the library's resources. Likewise, families who only visited the library for storytimes were staying in the library for lunch before heading home. It quickly became apparent that summer reading and Lunch at the Library were not, in fact, two separate programs. Parents and families did not see a separation of services between the two programs; they were entwined in their minds. And so they became entwined in the minds of library staff as well. In Ontario as in so many other California libraries, summer reading is Lunch at the Library, and Lunch at the Library is summer reading.

In summer 2016, project consultant Virginia Walter and project manager Trish Garone conducted observations of programs at the Chula Vista Public Library, Fresno County Public Library, Los Angeles Public Library, Sacramento Public Library, Oakland Public Library, and the San Diego Public Library. They noted:

> "The programs are not only providing meals for the children and teens in our communities who need them. They are engaging children, teens, and families with learning and enrichment opportunities, exposing children and teens to new foods, providing families with opportunities for social interaction with a diverse group of people, fostering new friendships, providing structure to the day, and giving people a feeling of pride in their community and its libraries. A mother at Fresno Central Library who described herself as a community activist, said that the library did a better job than any other agency of making people feel at home during the meal. She said, 'It doesn't feel like charity here.'"[16]

California's summer meal programs bring new families to the library in addition to providing meals for library regulars, and they provide staff with opportunities to introduce families to library services and resources. In 2013, at Fresno's Central Library, summer reading participation rose nearly 19 percent from the previous year—to 988 participants. Library staff said:

> "I believe the increase has to do with the summer lunch program and people learning about all the different services the library has to offer."

In the same year, 355 people took part in summer reading as a result of the Lunch at the Library program at the Los Angeles Public Library. Library staff said:

> "We signed a lot of kids up for summer reading and succeeded in helping parents see the library as a place that is multifaceted in its approach to serving families."

The Sacramento Public Library's Valley Hi-North Laguna Branch saw its summer reading program participation almost triple from 2012 to 2013, from 744 to 2,110 participants. In addition, the branch experienced a 6.6 percent increase in the issuance of new library cards over the previous year. The library did not hold a library card drive in 2013, and it credits the meal program as the driving force for the increase. Staff said:

> "The summer meals program at Valley Hi-North Laguna was nothing short of transformational."

The program is also helping to resolve behavioral issues among regular library patrons by addressing the often-hidden issue of hunger in the community. It is well-documented that hunger can impact attention, concentration, and behavior, and thus academic readiness. Participating librarians have observed the summer meal program providing benefits to library regulars. They see improved behavior and attentiveness, and a "sense of calm," among children at their libraries and have attributed the improvement to the lunch element.

Lunch at the Library Project Outcomes

Librarians in California have developed outcome statements in order to help library staff plan, present, evaluate, and demonstrate the value of their summer meal programs. California's Lunch at the Library outcomes are:

1. Families know they can get help and essential resources at the library.
2. Families feel healthy, happy, and safe.

The outcomes are designed to help ensure that California's public library summer meal programs fulfill their potential by connecting children, teens, and adults with libraries' services and resources and helping to foster positive well-being among participating families. Providing food for hungry children and teens is important and valuable work by itself, but the outcomes encourage library staff to extend the program's impact by taking full advantage of the library environment in order to provide families with an enriching and impactful experience along with the meal service.

California library staff have designed their summer meal programs to achieve the stated outcomes, and as a result of these efforts, California's public library summer meal programs are successfully introducing families to libraries' services and resources and helping families feel healthy, both physically and emotionally. Moreover, California library staff have collected data that demonstrate the impact and value of their program.

In 2016, survey results showed that families taking part in California's public library summer meal program know they can get help and essential resources at the library—an important finding when so many of the families who visit the library for summer meals are not library regulars:

- 90 percent of people surveyed know they can find books and things to borrow at the library;[17]
- 66 percent know they can find people to help them;
- 63 percent know they can find things to make and play with;
- 65 percent know they can find information;
- 75 percent know they can find access to computers; and
- 71 percent know they can take part in summer reading.

Participating families also reported that they felt healthy, happy, and safe:

- 66 percent feel good about themselves;
- 60 percent feel safe; and
- 79 percent feel happy.

Families tell us:

"I would like to thank everyone for helping me learn to read, eat, and feel safe."

"It's just nice to be part of a program that all-around cares."

"[This program makes me] feel like the community cares about us."

"The lunch program is wonderful and has been a big help to our family. [We're] struggling financially—thank you and God bless."

"It's a great program. It motivates the children to come back and check out books."

The surveys we use to capture evaluation data can be found in the appendix. They are designed to be used with children, teens, and adults, and to be administered easily during the busy summer period, and they have proven to be successful in capturing data from families. We invite other libraries to adopt our outcomes and use our survey tools and resources to develop effective programs, demonstrate program value, and improve program quality.

Best Practices

California's librarians have launched their summer meal programs with a combination of enthusiasm, excitement, trepidation, and caution. There are plenty of legitimate things to worry about, ranging from how the program will work during the already busy summer months, convincing administrators and staff that this is really and truly a great idea, and following the many rules of USDA summer meal programs, to the myriad "what ifs" of things that just might go wrong. However, libraries' passion for and commitment to their communities have outweighed the anxiety. Their efforts have paid off, and California's programs have generated a number of success stories and best practices that can guide the development of summer meal programs in any community.

1. KNOW THE BASICS

It is important to be clear about program fundamentals before getting started.

The USDA's summer nutrition programs, more commonly referred to as summer meal programs, ensure that children and youth in low-income neighborhoods continue to have access to healthy food when school lets out for summer vacation. They enable school districts, units of local government, tribal governments, and community-based agencies to offer free, healthy meals to children and youth aged eighteen and under in low-income neighborhoods. They are offered in all fifty states and administered by state agencies; in California, the program is administered and overseen by the California Department of Education's Nutrition Services Division. Meal services must comply with requirements specified by the USDA and the state agency.

The summer meal *site,* such as the library, is the physical location where the meals will be served. Site staff are tasked with handling and serving meals; monitoring food to ensure it complies with health and safety regulations and other program rules, such as tracking the number of meals served; and record-keeping. While libraries may be eligible to act as both a sponsor and a site, California public libraries typically serve as summer meal sites. Libraries typically operate as "open" sites in contrast to an enrolled summer program, which may operate as a "closed enrolled site." If security or space become a concern once the meal program has started, libraries may discuss the option of becoming a "restricted open site" with their sponsor. At open sites like libraries, meals are served to all children without requiring parents or caregivers to complete any paperwork.

The summer meal *sponsor,* which is often a school district, city or county agency, or nonprofit organization (for example, the YMCA), acts as the administrative and fiscal agent for the program. The sponsor provides the meals that are served at the site. Sponsoring agencies are reimbursed by the USDA for providing meals that meet federal nutrition guidelines outlined in the program and are designed specifically to serve children ages eighteen and under.

Because summer meal programs are designed to serve areas with high populations of economically disadvantaged children, libraries should begin by looking to see if their building is located in an eligible area. Branch staff may know anecdotally that the library is serving a low-income neighborhood, but for the library to become a summer meal site this belief must be substantiated. Libraries can confirm their neighborhood's eligibility through the Food Research & Action Center's Summer Food Mapper, the USDA's Capacity Builder Tool, and by contacting their local state administering agency.[18] Typically, eligibility is determined using local school data or census data, stipulating that sites are eligible if at least 50 percent of the children in the local area are eligible for free or reduced-price lunches.

Once libraries have established that they are located in an eligible neighborhood, they should consider whether they have the space and staffing resources to take on this effort. Careful assessment and planning around capacity and needs is required to ensure the program's success. California libraries are successfully providing summer meal programs in spaces that range from community rooms with attached kitchens to out in the library among the stacks. The program can be offered in very small spaces, but library staff must determine whether their library can successfully implement the program in the space available. When having conversations about library capacity, all relevant staff members should be included to ensure that all voices are heard and a variety of perspectives is considered. If becoming a summer meal site does not seem feasible right away, consider connecting with a local summer meal provider to support other summer meal sites out in the community, for example, at a local park, until the library is more prepared.

We recommend that libraries draw on resources available online to learn about program basics and all best practices before getting started. Resources are available, among other places, at www.lunchatthelibrary.org and at the USDA and FRAC websites.[19]

2. INVOLVE EVERYONE

Summer meal programs are whole-family, whole-library programs, and the most successful engage a variety of staff members in program planning, implementation, evaluation, and reflection. Summer meal programs are nontraditional programs, and staff are more likely to be supportive if they are involved from the start and if their concerns are heard and addressed.

Libraries should not be tempted to make the summer meal program a task for youth services staff alone—not least because summer is already their busiest time of year. Summer meal programs bring families to the library, and they provide all library staff with opportunities to connect with adults as well as children and teens.

During the summer, all staff should know where lunches are being served, so they can let families know about the service and direct them to it. To help enhance and strengthen the connection that families make with the library during the meal service, make sure that staff are on hand to make connections with families. When no library staff are present, the personal contact with the librarian who works with children and families is missed. The program can also provide a great opportunity for the staff in large libraries to get to know one another. We have seen the summer meal program contribute to staff development when staff from different departments volunteer to serve meals, side by side, in the community room.

3. START WITH EVALUATION

Anyone planning a summer meal program should focus on evaluation at the start of the planning period to ensure that the summer meal program is designed to achieve stated outcomes, goals, and objectives.

Libraries should set outcomes that are relevant to their community, and they should create programs that are designed to achieve those outcomes. Whether libraries develop their own local outcomes, or draw on the outcome statements developed in California, all staff and volunteers should be aware of the outcome statements and should be working to achieve them. Evaluation tools should be designed and administered to discover whether the outcomes are achieved.

Output data are important, too. The USDA requires staff at summer meal sites to record how many meals are served each day and to report this information to their meal sponsors. These numbers—along with other output data such as numbers of enrichment programs and community partners—are an important part of the library's summer meal story, helping to demonstrate the need for the program and the breadth of impact the program is having.

All data, including photographs, should be combined to demonstrate program impact; help staff reflect on successes, challenges, and lessons learned; and improve program quality. A full set of data will help library staff paint a rich picture of the summer meal program that can be used to raise awareness of the library and demonstrate to stakeholders the impact of library services.

4. CREATE A WELCOMING AND INVITING SPACE

Meals should be served in an inviting space that will make families feel welcome and encourage them to return. A warm and welcoming space will help families feel healthy, happy, and safe, will help library staff successfully introduce families to the library's resources, and will encourage them to return to the library in the future.

Libraries are ideally suited to being open and welcoming summer meal sites for families. A recent study of summer meal programs in California's Silicon Valley reported that families described the library as "feeling like 'home.'" The study's authors stated that

> "the 'home-like' atmosphere conveyed by library staff was cited as one of the most positive aspects of the summer meal programme. Participants appreciated the library meal programme because library staff were friendly and everyone was welcome. The inclusive nature of libraries helped to reduce stigma among participants, as everyone at the library during the lunch period was able to receive a free meal regardless of income, age or immigration status. Stigma associated with participation in safety-net programmes such as [the Supplemental Nutrition Assistance Program] SNAP

has been found to be a major deterrent to programme participation, due to shame and disrespectful treatment when accessing services. The welcoming and stigma-free environment created by libraries is consistent with the library's inherent culture outlined in the Library Bill of Rights that states, 'A person's right to use a library should not be denied or abridged because of origin, age, background, or views.' The library culture effectively breaks down many of the traditional barriers to meal programme participation, making libraries ideal for addressing [food insecurity] in an environment where people from all backgrounds and socio-economic circumstances can eat together."[20]

Simple ideas for creating a welcoming space include displaying books and wall art, setting out passive programs that allow self-directed learning and enrichment, playing music, using attractive tablecloths, writing out a daily menu and placing it on the tables, and setting up manipulatives and other educational toys to help enhance the play and learning atmosphere. A librarian at the Los Angeles Public Library has reported that play kitchens were "ragingly popular with kids ages two to seven."

All volunteers should be trained in how to greet and work with families. In some libraries, volunteers take on the duty of being the official greeter. In others, librarians or the library director invite families to have lunch with them. The room should be staffed with people who can talk with families in the language they feel most comfortable using. These personal greetings contribute to an overall feeling of welcome and caring.

Always take the opportunity to engage one-on-one with the families in the lunchroom and make connections with previously underserved families as well as library regulars. Let them know about the library's services and resources and don't forget to issue them with library cards.

5. PROVIDE PROGRAMMING—FOR THE WHOLE FAMILY!

The most successful summer meal sites are those that offer programs and activities to complement the meal service. Libraries are ideally positioned to provide learning and enrichment activities before, during, and after lunch, and by offering high-quality programming alongside the meal service, libraries can help to prevent summer learning loss as well as food insecurity in low-income neighborhoods. Furthermore, as one librarian has noted:

"[The summer meal program] successfully linked healthy meals to summer reading and active play. [It] expanded everyone's ideas of what happens at a library."

The key to providing meaningful programming is to have staff available to plan, implement, evaluate, and then change the programs if necessary.

The wide variety of activities at California's public library summer meal programs includes storytimes, craft stations, art and writing workshops, Zumba, ping-pong, nutrition education programs, bike-blender smoothie-making, container gardening, coloring and activity sheets, yoga, make-it-and-take-it tables, board games, pedestrian safety workshops, chalk and rock constellation-making, book talks, and much more. Libraries often need to experiment with a range of activities to determine the type of programming that is the best fit for them, given the drop-in context, available staffing, and space. The Los Angeles Public Library has had great success with STEAM activity stations in the lunchrooms. The stations have enabled kids to plant and grow seeds, explore weight and measurement, investigate rocks with magnifying glasses, study magnets, build ramps, and predict distance and speed. The library has made different activities available each day throughout the summer and given kids the opportunity to create experiments, make predictions, and record observations. The San Diego County Library has offered a popular "App Academy," enabling kids to use learning-based apps on iPads during the lunch program. The Oakland Public Library has partnered with the Oakland Museum of Modern Art for several years to bring high-quality art experiences to the library and provide families with opportunities to work and learn alongside local artists.

Summer meal programs provide libraries with a great opportunity to give books to families to keep in the home. Stephen Krashen's research has demonstrated that proximity and easy access to books are a critical factor in children's development of reading skills.[21] The Fresno County Public Library has contracted with a local nonprofit organization, Reading and Beyond, to provide literacy enrichment sessions at lunch sites, and in 2016 they also distributed 5,000 books at their summer meal sites.

Because summer meal programs often bring whole families to the library, they provide library staff with opportunities to engage parents and other caregivers while their children are eating lunch. The Los Angeles Public Library successfully partnered with Los Angeles Universal Preschool (LAUP), a Los Angeles-based early education nonprofit, to conduct a pilot intervention that introduced parents and children to LAUP's "Take Time. Talk!" language tool.

The pilot project aimed to support early language development in low-income populations, and the results showed that parents learned and retained the information they heard about "Take Time. Talk!" and that they used, or intended to use, the tool with their children.[22]

The learning and enrichment element can be introduced slowly without compromising the overall quality of the summer meal program. In their first year, libraries often prefer to focus on creating an inviting space, connecting families with the summer reading program, and offering passive programming while staff get used to the meal service and get to know participating families. Families often return for lunch day after day, which provides staff with a great opportunity to help them complete the summer reading program and keep reading all summer long. Year two—once staff and volunteers are comfortable serving meals—can be a great time to start introducing programming that is tailored to the needs of the families who come to the library for lunch.

6. FOOD BRINGS PEOPLE (AND PARTNERS) TOGETHER

California's public library summer meal programs have fostered meaningful partnerships and elevated the library's profile as an important community partner when school is out. Libraries' primary summer meal partners are the meal sponsors who provide the meals each day and who promote the library through their own networks. In some communities, libraries and meal sponsors have also worked together on citywide summer kickoff events, and sponsors have provided staff to help operate the meal service at the library.

In California, meal sponsors have appreciated that libraries have adeptly followed the many program rules and reported that libraries were among their most well-attended sites. Some libraries and meal sponsors have extended their partnerships to include new projects such as providing meals to students during homework clubs and other after-school programs and developing joint collaborations with other city and county agencies.

Several California libraries have partnered with an organization called Vision to Learn, which provides free vision screening and eyeglasses to children in low-income neighborhoods. Vision to Learn's mobile screening unit, which would otherwise have gone unused in the absence of school, visits libraries to test kids' vision and distribute eyeglasses during the meal service. One librarian said:

"Families lined up early when the Vision to Learn bus came to Central and many of them had to wait two hours to get examined. They remained cheerful in the hot sun—and when the glasses came the day before school started and we called all the families, they ALL picked them up that very day! Now all these kids can see the blackboard."

Community collaborations have enabled libraries to offer a range of programming that did not require significant, if any, additional funds, and have enabled them to tap into other community resources. These types of partnerships have also meant that libraries did not need to stray from their already-planned summer schedules when starting the meal service, but could add supplementary activities as needed.

At the Riverside County Library System's Glen Avon Regional Library, dental exams were provided by Miles of Smiles, a program offered through the Riverside Community Health Foundation. In Solano County, the library provided families with opportunities to learn more about registering with the CalFresh program from the Food Bank of Contra Costa and Solano, Medi-Cal registration and information from the Solano Coalition for Better Health, service referrals from the Solano County Health and Social Service Mental Health unit, and the Solano Kids Insurance Program (Covered California) from the Solano Coalition for Better Health. In San Diego County, the library partnered with the local health and human services agency to offer "Instant Recess" physical activities to keep kids moving. Firefighters, congressional representatives, locally elected leaders, and the police chief have read stories to kids during the lunch service at Contra Costa County's San Pablo branch library. And in many communities, partnerships with local health departments have enabled libraries to offer nutrition education alongside the lunch service. Community partners have been eager to work with the libraries because they, too, have needed a vehicle to reach families and promote their services when school is out.

Rural Areas

Partnerships have been particularly crucial in rural areas, which face the added summertime burden of transportation issues, extreme heat, a smaller pool of organizational partners to work with, and sometimes a complete shutdown of schools which limits summer learning opportunities as well as summer meals. In Borrego Springs, a small town located two hours outside of San Diego, kids had very few summer options. The library partnered with the school district, the community pool, a local Boys and Girls Club, and community partners to combine resources to transport kids to different activities throughout the day, landing at the library for lunch and programming in the middle of the day. Part of the San Diego County Library, the Borrego Springs Branch Library received meals through Feeding America San Diego, a local food bank. In addition, a food bank volunteer, impressed with the collaboration, drove weekly to the library to supply bags of produce (provided through the food bank's produce program) for the children to bring home to their families.

Perhaps the most significant outcome of these partnerships is how they helped libraries, partners, and local leaders think more broadly about leveraging summer meal programs in order to help their communities work smarter and more collaboratively. After reading to children in Kern County's Beale Memorial Library and seeing firsthand the value of the program, a county supervisor became one of the program's biggest champions. In San Pablo, a local council member supported the program by regularly visiting the library to read to children and by helping to facilitate relationships with other agencies and leaders. From a local leader's perspective, Lunch at the Library illustrates a best-case scenario: city or county agencies working together effectively to support the community.

7. VOLUNTEERISM TURNED YOUTH DEVELOPMENT OPPORTUNITY

Volunteers are essential to the success of library meal programs, and libraries' experience and expertise in recruiting and working with volunteers has contributed to their success as summer meal sites. Volunteers have been invaluable for library staff already stretched thin with summer reading programs and activities, and regulars often provide continuity for the program throughout the summer months.

Because it is mandatory that summer meal sites adhere to state and federal regulations, libraries must ensure that volunteers understand program rules and regulations. Volunteers who will be working with families should also receive good training in how to be welcoming and friendly, interact with families, implement the regulations sensitively, provide information about the library, and serve as library advocates out in the community.

While volunteers of all ages typically do a great job organizing and presenting the lunch program, they will get the most out of their experience and will contribute most to the program when they are well-trained and when they work on tasks that are best suited to their personalities and skill sets. A shy teen might prefer and might be better-equipped to design promotional flyers than greet families or read stories to children.

Teens are commonly used as volunteers in California's public library summer meal programs. They have been recruited through schools, community agencies such as Boys and Girls Clubs, library volunteer programs, library regulars, teens looking for community service hours, and teen-to-teen word of mouth. In Sacramento, the coordinating librarian said:

> "More teens then joined through word of mouth because of the positive environment. They came to work and hang out with their friends."

Teen volunteers have helped to plan meal services, greet families, hand out meals, manage meal service logistics, and engage children and their families with activities. In Contra Costa County Library's San Pablo Branch Library, teen volunteers designed their own nutrition education game to promote healthy eating and engage younger children in physical activity in addition to helping manage the meal program. Most teen volunteers have come from the community that is being served and many are already skilled in working with younger children, thanks to having siblings of their own. Teens and young adults are indispensable assets to the program, and library staff have seen the program engage teens and spark a passion among them. In Los Angeles, library staff have said:

> "The teen volunteers—in particular, one girl who came regularly every day—were essential. Because we had such a big group of staff working summer lunch, there were many people who only worked one day a week, and so we were constantly training and reminding them about procedures. The volunteers, because they were there every day, provided continuity and stability for the families—and often told staff what they needed to be doing."

More than simply providing community service, teens are acquiring organization, management, communication, and teamwork skills that are crucial for a twenty-first-century workforce. As a bonus, they are also able to eat the meals being served. In Los Angeles, the library has paid for teens to obtain food handling certificates, which will add to their employer desirability should they choose to pursue jobs in the food service industry. In Sacramento, a volunteer coordinator hosted a workshop to help teens identify and articulate the skills they learned while volunteering at the meal program, discussed strategies for pursuing a job, and provided sample resumes and letters of recommendation. The coordinator arranged for the human resources personnel at Target and the executive vice president of a local technology company to give presentations at the volunteer appreciation lunch held at the conclusion of the summer, and library staff said:

> "That Lunch at the Library turned into a training ground for the teens was an unexpected bonus."

8. PUBLICITY, PROMOTION, AND OUTREACH: BE READY FOR MEDIA

Families need to know about the summer meal program for it to be successful, so be sure to create an outreach plan. Library users and non-users are both part of the target audience, so the program should be promoted both in the library and out in the community. Partners, including the meal sponsors, can help promote the lunch program to their communities and stakeholders. In California, programs have grown very quickly by word of mouth, and any libraries that are concerned about capacity might start by implementing just a few outreach strategies and monitoring program growth from there. Typically, traditional outreach methods (such as posting flyers, providing information to schools, partners, and community leaders, and notifying local media) have been enough for libraries to develop popular and thriving lunch programs.

The relative novelty of offering food in the library has helped generate significant media attention for libraries, helping to raise awareness about food insecurity, summer learning loss, and library services, and augmenting library efforts to promote the service to families. Library staff should be prepared for media inquiries, prepare the points they want to get across, and take this opportunity to highlight the library's programs and resources and the impact they have in the community. Let everyone know how great your library is!

It Wouldn't Be Perfect without a Few Flaws

Even the most perfect diamond has a few flaws. The Lunch at the Library project has demonstrated that a summer meal program can be transformative for libraries in many ways. It has also exposed a range of challenges, some of which can be addressed by libraries and others that require larger, systematic changes.

The primary concerns reported by librarians are related to USDA summer nutrition program regulations. Because summer meal programs are designed specifically to serve children and youth, there is no flexibility to also offer their adult caregivers a free meal. Although the adults seem to understand that this is a regulation that cannot be sidestepped, it can sometimes be challenging for staff, volunteers, and families, and is awkward at best. The regulation can be emotionally difficult for staff and volunteers in areas where adult food insecurity is an issue and in an institution that prides itself on access for all. Eating meals together as a family can facilitate children's healthy eating habits and is an integral part of many, if not most, cultures. Many libraries are exploring opportunities to provide free meals to caregivers by partnering with food banks or other community agencies to provide fruits, vegetables, and other snacks for adults. Some meal sponsors will sell meals to parents at a low cost, and some libraries have purchased food for adults from their library's budget.

Where libraries can provide food for caregivers, the summer meal program will have greater impact. Researchers who observed the Silicon Valley programs said:

> "Since the library meal programmes in the present study provided meals to both children and adults, participants discussed an overall feeling of inclusiveness as a result of the adult meals. Parent and adult participants valued the ability to eat with children and other community members. Parent participants specifically noted that eating with their children strengthened family bonds. Even adult participants who did not have children appreciated the family atmosphere that the library meal programme fostered."[23]

Whether or not the library is able to provide food for adults, we recommend that summer meal sites provide information on where adults can obtain free or low-cost healthy food in the community. We also suggest that libraries prominently display the USDA regulations stating that only children and teens may receive its free lunches, display them in multiple languages, and in an easy-to-understand way in the meal service room. These steps can help raise awareness among participating families and help alleviate uncomfortable situations for patrons or library staff and volunteers.

In some libraries, food quality is a concern. In cases where menus became repetitive or food items were not well liked, libraries have worked with their food partners to make improvements where possible. Libraries can also serve as great places for school districts to test new lunch menu items and get feedback from children. USDA summer meal programs operate through a reimbursement mechanism, and providers must work within those funding constraints to provide food that is both healthy and appealing. Regulations require that (with some exceptions) all food must be consumed on-site, which can also create a food waste issue for food that is not consumed. While some libraries have been able to find workable solutions with their providers, such as having fewer meals sent to the site, working with food recovery organizations, or improving quality, the issue remains one of greater significance within the food system. It is also a reminder of the unsolvable problem of finding the "right" amount of food for each individual child in a program designed to feed many.

Some libraries have also had internal challenges to address: How would staff feel about being asked to do "one more thing" during what can be the busiest time of the year? Would library administration be supportive of the program in order to help ensure effective implementation? Was there really need in the community? Would this program be perceived as an effort *only* for the children's librarian? How would other staff see this as part of their job too? Not surprisingly, exposure has been a key strategy to alleviating anxiety and resistance where these existed: providing staff and leadership with firsthand experience of the program enabled them to see its value, both to the community and the library. It has also been helpful for all library staff to understand in advance that in many communities, the face of poverty has changed and "need" is not always overtly visible. The meal service has provided many librarians with an opportunity to sit down with families and hear their stories, building a deeper relationship with the community.

Bringing It All Together

The Lunch at the Library project is a perfect example of the transformation of summer in California's public libraries. Through their public library summer meal programs, libraries are reaching out to previously underserved members of the community and engaging them with summer programming and with the variety of other services and resources that libraries provide. Libraries are taking an outcome-based approach to program planning and evaluation. They are fostering community and connections and providing summer program participants with value and enjoyment. Through the lunch program they are building strong communities, providing opportunities for learning, celebrating reading and literacy, and creating programs that are designed to reach and engage everyone. Moreover, they are bringing together community-based agencies and organizations to work collaboratively to address learning loss and food insecurity in the summer months.

Notes

1. Natalie Cole and Patrice Chamberlain, "Nourishing Bodies & Minds When School Is Out: California's Public Library Summer Meal Programs," *Public Libraries* 54, no. 2 (April 2015): 22–28.

2. No Kid Hungry Center for Best Practices, "Share Our Strength: Summer Meals Survey" (March 2013), https://bestpractices.nokidhungry.org/sites/default/files/resources/SOS%20-%20Summer%20Meals%20Survey%20Report%20FINAL2.pdf.

3. Harris Cooper, Barbara Nye, Kelly Charlton, James Lindsay, and Scott Greathouse, "The Effects of Summer Vacation on Achievement Test Scores: A Narrative and Meta-Analytic Review," *Review of Educational Research* 66, no. 3 (Autumn 1996): 227–68.

4. Summer Matters, "Why Summer Matters," www.packard.org/wp-content/uploads/2017/02/Why-Summer-Matters-Infographic.pdf.

5. Karl L. Alexander, Doris R. Entwisle, and Linda Steffel Olson, "Lasting Consequences of the Summer Learning Gap," *American Sociological Review* 72, no. 2 (April 2007): 167–80.

6. Paul T. von Hippel, Brian Powell, Douglas B. Downey, and Nicholas J. Rowland, "The Effect of School on Overweight in Childhood: Gains in Body Mass Index during the School Year and during Summer Vacation," *American Journal of Public Health* 97, no. 4 (April 2007): 692–704; Brenda McLaughlin, "Healthy Summers for Kids: Turning Risk into Opportunity" (National Summer Learning Association, May 2012), http://c.ymcdn.com/sites/www.summerlearning.org/resource/resmgr/Healthy_Summers_/NSLA_Healthy_Summers_for_Kid.pdf.

7. Amy Bohnert, Nicole Zarrett, Michael W. Beets, Georgia Hall, Joanna Buscemi, Amy Heard, and Russell Pate, "Curbing Summertime Weight Gain among America's Youth" (*Society of Behavioral Medicine*, February 2017), www.sbm.org/UserFiles/file/CurbingYouthSummerWeightGain_forweb.pdf.

8. Diana F. Jyoti, Edward A. Frongillo, and Sonya J. Jones, "Food Insecurity Affects School Children's Academic Performance, Weight Gain, and Social Skills," *Journal of Nutrition* 135, no. 12 (December 1, 2005): 2831–39.

9. Joan Luby, Andy Belden, Kelly Botteron, Natasha Marrus, Michael P. Harms, Casey Babb, Tomoyuki Nishino, and Deanna Barch, "The Effects of Poverty on Childhood Brain Development: The Mediating Effect of Caregiving and Stressful Life Events," *JAMA Pediatrics* 167, no. 12 (December 2013): 1135–42.

10. Food Research & Action Center, "National School Lunch Program," http://frac.org/programs/national-school-lunch-program.

11. Clarissa Hayes, Randy Rosso, Signe Anderson, and Crystal FitzSimons, "Hunger Doesn't Take a Vacation: Summer Nutrition Status Report" (Food Research & Action Center, June 2016), 3, http://frac.org/wp-content/uploads/2016_summer_nutrition_report.pdf.

12. Ibid.

13. California Food Policy Advocates, "School's Out . . . Who Ate? Data Highlights" (July 9, 2013), http://cfpa.net/ChildNutrition/Summer/CFPAPublications/SOWA -DataHighlights-2013.pdf.

14. Kathy Rosa, ed., "The State of America's Libraries: A Report from the American Library Association: 2015" (American Library Association, 2015), www.ala.org/news/sites/ ala.org.news/files/content/0415_StateAmLib_0.pdf.

15. Kathryn Zickuhr, Lee Rainie, Kristen Purcell, and Maeve Duggan, "How Americans Value Public Libraries in Their Communities" (Pew Research Center, December 11, 2013), http://libraries.pewinternet.org/files/legacy-pdf/PIP_Libraries%20in%20 communities.pdf.

16. Virginia A. Walter and Patricia Garone, "Summer Lunch @ Your Library: Lessons Learned" (report submitted to the California Library Association, December 2016).

17. In total, 5,121 people in 73 libraries completed surveys in 2016.

18. Food Research & Action Center, "Summer Food Mapper," http://frac.org/research/ resource-library/summer-food-mapper; United States Department of Agriculture, Food and Nutrition Service, "Capacity Builder," www.fns.usda.gov/ capacitybuilder.

19. California Library Association, "Lunch at the Library," http://lunchatthelibrary.org/; Food Research & Action Center, "Summer Nutrition Programs," http://frac.org/ programs/summer-nutrition-programs; United States Department of Agriculture, Food and Nutrition Service, "Summer Food Service Program," www.fns.usda.gov/ sfsp/summer-food-service-program.

20. Janine S. Bruce, Monica M. De La Cruz, Gala Moreno, and Lisa J. Chamberlain, "Lunch at the Library: Examination of a Community-Based Approach to Addressing Summer Food Insecurity," *Public Health Nutrition,* 20, no. 9 (June 2017): 1640–49, doi: 10.1017/S1368980017000258.

21. Stephen D. Krashen, *The Power of Reading: Insights from the Research,* 2nd ed. (West- port, CT: Libraries Unlimited, 2004).

22. Melissa Barnhart and Mariel Kyger, "Take Time. Talk! An Intervention to Improve Early Language Development in Low-Income Populations" (presented at the 2016 Child Health, Education, and Care Summit, Sacramento, CA, November 9, 2016), www.ccfc.ca.gov/pdf/about/annual_conference/2016_Sessions/1K-Take% 20Time.%20Talk!.pdf.

23. Bruce et al., "Lunch at the Library," 8.

CONCLUSION

The Never-Ending Story

The transformation of California's public library summer programs is an ongoing process. Our goal is for library staff in all of California's public libraries to provide strong and effective summer programs that build strong communities, provide opportunities for learning, celebrate reading and literacy, and that are designed to reach and engage everyone. The story we have told here describes our progress so far and points in the direction we are headed.

To achieve our goal and ensure that California's programs continue to transform and stay relevant, the Summer @ Your Library project will continue to support and expand the initiatives and resources included in this book—such as outcome- and outreach-based planning and evaluation, partnerships between public libraries and school- and community-based summer learning programs, and the Lunch at the Library program—and we will continue to develop new resources that align with the aspirations of our communities.

New Directions

Partnerships will continue to evolve. We recently built on a relationship that the California State Library's early literacy initiative, Early Learning with Families, had developed with the Bay Area Discovery Museum's Center for Childhood Creativity (CCC). The result is a guide and training based on the CCC's unique pedagogical framework, the CREATE framework, that supports library staff in learning how they can develop children's creative problem-solving through intentional experiences.

To help libraries connect underserved communities with their summer programs, we are currently working with a small group of libraries in San Diego, Los Angeles, Richmond, and Butte County to explore how libraries can engage more families with summer reading by developing partnerships with housing authorities.

Growing out of the work that started with the Summer Matters campaign, the California State Library is represented on the California Department of Education's Summer Learning Implementation Committee, which is making recommendations for building the capacity of the System of Support for Expanded Learning in California. In the Greater Los Angeles region, librarians are working collaboratively with educators and other expanded learning providers to enhance summer programming opportunities for youth.

The Lunch at the Library program continues to expand. Moving forward, Summer @ Your Library project staff will work with libraries to extend their summer meal programs by offering after-school meals. We will explore the different ways libraries can offer summer meals, such as on their bookmobiles, and we will provide support to library staff who take summer programming out to summer meal sites at parks and other community locations.

We will continue to provide library staff with opportunities to convene at conferences, trainings, regional and online meetings, and use social media to strengthen the developing community of practices across the state. The informal community of practice that has emerged from these gatherings is one of the most valuable consequences of the transformation process.

The future is always unknown, of course. However, Summer @ Your Library will continue to transform.

APPENDIX

Surveys

Early Childhood

Outcome statement: Young children and their caregivers feel part of a community of readers and library users.

Survey Questions:

1. We feel welcome at the library

   ☐ *Agree strongly*　☐ *Agree*　☐ *Disagree*　☐ *Disagree strongly*　☐ *Don't know*

2. We took part in activities at the library during the summer

   ☐ *Agree strongly*　☐ *Agree*　☐ *Disagree*　☐ *Disagree strongly*　☐ *Don't know*

3. We enjoyed the summer reading program

   ☐ *Agree strongly*　☐ *Agree*　☐ *Disagree*　☐ *Disagree strongly*　☐ *Don't know*

4. We enjoy books that we borrow from the library

   ☐ *Agree strongly*　☐ *Agree*　☐ *Disagree*　☐ *Disagree strongly*　☐ *Don't know*

5. We plan to come back to the library after the summer

   ☐ *Agree strongly*　☐ *Agree*　☐ *Disagree*　☐ *Disagree strongly*　☐ *Don't know*

6. Is this the first time your child took part in the summer reading program?

   ☐ *Yes*　☐ *No, we have taken part before*　☐ *Don't know*

School-Age Children

Outcome statement: Children feel part of a community of readers and library users.

Survey Questions:

1. I feel good at the library

   ☐ *Agree strongly*   ☐ *Agree*   ☐ *Disagree*   ☐ *Disagree strongly*   ☐ *Don't know*

2. I took part in activities at the library during the summer

   ☐ *Agree strongly*   ☐ *Agree*   ☐ *Disagree*   ☐ *Disagree strongly*   ☐ *Don't know*

3. I enjoyed the summer reading program

   ☐ *Agree strongly*   ☐ *Agree*   ☐ *Disagree*   ☐ *Disagree strongly*   ☐ *Don't know*

4. I talk about the books I read

   ☐ *Agree strongly*   ☐ *Agree*   ☐ *Disagree*   ☐ *Disagree strongly*   ☐ *Don't know*

5. I plan to come back to the library after the summer

   ☐ *Agree strongly*   ☐ *Agree*   ☐ *Disagree*   ☐ *Disagree strongly*   ☐ *Don't know*

6. Is this the first time you took part in the summer reading program?

   ☐ *Yes*   ☐ *No, I have taken part before*   ☐ *Don't know*

Teens

Outcome statement: Teens make connections at the library.

Survey Questions:

1. I feel welcome at the library

   ☐ *Agree strongly*   ☐ *Agree*   ☐ *Disagree*   ☐ *Disagree strongly*   ☐ *Don't know*

2. I spent time with other people at the library this summer

   ☐ *Agree strongly*   ☐ *Agree*   ☐ *Disagree*   ☐ *Disagree strongly*   ☐ *Don't know*

3. What did you discover at the library this summer? (Add examples; for example: new books, teen events, ideas, friends)?

   Please tell us: _____

   _____

   _____

4. I enjoyed spending time at the library during the summer

☐ *Agree strongly*   ☐ *Agree*   ☐ *Disagree*   ☐ *Disagree strongly*   ☐ *Don't know*

5. I plan to return to the library after the summer

☐ *Agree strongly*   ☐ *Agree*   ☐ *Disagree*   ☐ *Disagree strongly*   ☐ *Don't know*

6. Is this the first time you took part in the summer reading program?

☐ *Yes*   ☐ *No, I have taken part before*   ☐ *Don't know*

Adults

Outcome statement: Adults find value and enjoyment at their library.

Survey Questions:

1. I feel welcome at the library

☐ *Agree strongly*   ☐ *Agree*   ☐ *Disagree*   ☐ *Disagree strongly*   ☐ *Don't know*

2. The library is valuable to me

☐ *Agree strongly*   ☐ *Agree*   ☐ *Disagree*   ☐ *Disagree strongly*   ☐ *Don't know*

Please tell us why: _____

_____

_____

3. The library is valuable to my community

☐ *Agree strongly*   ☐ *Agree*   ☐ *Disagree*   ☐ *Disagree strongly*   ☐ *Don't know*

4. I enjoyed spending time at the library during the summer

☐ *Agree strongly*   ☐ *Agree*   ☐ *Disagree*   ☐ *Disagree strongly*   ☐ *Don't know*

Please tell us why: _____

_____

_____

5. I plan to return to the library after the summer

☐ *Agree strongly*   ☐ *Agree*   ☐ *Disagree*   ☐ *Disagree strongly*   ☐ *Don't know*

6. Is this the first time you took part in the summer reading program?

☐ *Yes*   ☐ *No, I have taken part before*   ☐ *Don't know*

Lunch at the Library

Please circle the best answers or fill in the blanks. Please be honest. Your answers will help us improve the library. There are no right or wrong answers! Thank you for your help.

1. How old are you?

2. Which of these can you find at the library? Please check all that apply.

☐ *Books and other things to borrow*   ☐ *Things to make and play with*

☐ *Information*   ☐ *Friends*

☐ *People to help you*   ☐ *Volunteer opportunities*

☐ *Summer reading program*   ☐ *Other? Please tell us:*

☐ *Computers*   _____

☐ *Jobs for kids*   _____

3. How do you feel right now? Please check all that apply.

☐ *Good about myself*   ☐ *Calm*

☐ *Strong*   ☐ *Other? Please tell us:*

☐ *Happy*   _____

☐ *Safe*   _____

☐ *Important*   _____

4. Have you signed up for the library's summer reading program?

☐ *Yes*   ☐ *No*   ☐ *Don't know*

5. Where else do you get lunch over the summer?

_____

_____

_____

6. Tell us or draw a picture of something you liked or learned today at the library.

_____

_____

_____

7. Is there anything else you would like to tell us about the library or the library lunch program?

_____

_____

_____

_____

_____

_____

BIBLIOGRAPHY

Alexander, Karl L., Doris R. Entwisle, and Linda Steffel Olson. "Lasting Consequences of the Summer Learning Gap." *American Sociological Review* 72, no. 2 (April 2007): 167–80.

Allington, Richard L., and Anne McGill-Franzen. "Got Books?" *Educational Leadership* 65, no. 7 (April 2008): 20–23.

———, eds. *Summer Reading: Closing the Rich/Poor Reading Achievement Gap.* New York: Teachers College Press, 2012.

———, "Summer Reading Loss." In *Summer Reading: Closing the Rich/Poor Reading Achievement Gap,* 1–19. New York: Teachers College Press, 2012.

American Academy of Pediatrics. Council on Communications and Media. "Media and Young Minds." *Pediatrics* 138, no. 5 (November 2016): e20162591. doi: 10.1542/peds.2016–2591.

———, "Media Use by Children Younger Than 2 Years." *Pediatrics* 128, no. 5 (November 2011): 1040–45. doi: 10.1542/peds.2011–1753.

———, "Media Use in School-Aged Children and Adolescents." *Pediatrics* 138, no. 5 (November 2016): e20162592. doi: 10.1542/peds.2016–2592.

Annie E. Casey Foundation. "2015 KIDS COUNT Data Book: State Trends in Child Well-Being." 2015. www.aecf.org/m/resourcedoc/aecf-2015kidscountdatabook -2015.pdf.

Association for Library Service to Children. "ALSC Strategic Plan." February 2017. www.ala.org/alsc/aboutalsc/stratplan.

Barnhart, Melissa, and Mariel Kyger. "Take Time. Talk! An Intervention to Improve Early Language Development in Low-Income Populations." Presented at the 2016 Child Health, Education, and Care Summit, Sacramento, CA, November 9, 2016. www.ccfc.ca.gov/pdf/about/annual_conference/2016_Sessions/1K-Take%20Time.%20Talk!.pdf.

Barrette, Lydia Margaret. "Children's Reading Clubs: A Wise Plan." *Library Journal* 48, no. 17 (October 1, 1923): 816.

Bertin, Stephanie. "A History of Youth Summer Reading Programs in Public Libraries." MSLS thesis, School of Information and Library Science, University of North Carolina at Chapel Hill, 2004. https://ils.unc.edu/MSpapers/2977.pdf.

Bohnert, Amy, Nicole Zarrett, Michael W. Beets, Georgia Hall, Joanna Buscemi, Amy Heard, and Russell Pate. "Curbing Summertime Weight Gain among America's Youth." *Society of Behavioral Medicine*, February 2017. www.sbm.org/User Files/file/CurbingYouthSummerWeightGain_forweb.pdf.

Brandeis University. Heller School for Social Policy and Management. "diversity datakids.org California Profile." 2017. www.diversitydatakids.org/data/profile/3717/california.

Bruce, Janine S., Monica M. De La Cruz, Gala Moreno, and Lisa J. Chamberlain. "Lunch at the Library: Examination of a Community-Based Approach to Addressing Summer Food Insecurity." *Public Health Nutrition,* 20, no. 9 (June 2017): 1540–49, doi: 10.1017/S1368980017000258.

California Food Policy Advocates. "School's Out . . . Who Ate? Data Highlights." July 9, 2013. http://cfpa.net/ChildNutrition/Summer/CFPAPublications/SOWA -DataHighlights-2013.pdf.

California Library Association. "Lunch at the Library." http://lunchatthelibrary.org/.

———, "Summer @ Your Library: Explore, Learn, Read, Connect." http://calchallenge .org/impact/.

Chicago Public Library. "Reading for Credit." *Library Journal* 48, no. 13 (July 1923): 618.

Children's Defense Fund. "Children in the States." 2015. www.childrensdefense.org/library/data/state-data-repository/cits/2015/2015-children-in-the-states -complete.pdf.

Cole, Natalie, and Patrice Chamberlain. "Nourishing Bodies & Minds When School Is Out: California's Public Library Summer Meal Programs." *Public Libraries* 54, no. 2 (April 2015): 22–28.

Cole, Natalie, Virginia Walter, and Eva Mitnick. "Outcomes + Outreach: The California Summer Reading Outcomes Initiative." *Public Libraries* 52, no. 2 (March/April 2013): 38–43.

Common Sense Media. "Children, Teens, and Reading: A Common Sense Media Research Brief." 2014. www.commonsensemedia.org/research/children-teens -and-reading.

———, "Zero to Eight: Children's Media Use in America 2013." October 28, 2013. www.commonsensemedia.org/research/zero-to-eight-childrens-media-use-in -america-2013.

Cook, Ruth Cathlyn. "A Dozen Summer Programs Designed to Promote Retention in Young Children." *Elementary School Journal* 52, no. 7 (March 1952): 412–17.

Cooper, Harris, Kelly Charlton, Jeff C. Valentine, and Laura Muhlenbruck. "Making the Most of Summer School: A Meta-Analytic and Narrative Review." *Monographs of the Society for Research in Child Development* 65, no. 1 (2000): 1–127.

Cooper, Harris, Barbara Nye, Kelly Charlton, James Lindsay, and Scott Greathouse. "The Effects of Summer Vacation on Achievement Test Scores: A Narrative and Meta-Analytic Review." *Review of Educational Research* 66, no. 3 (Autumn 1996): 227–68.

Cushman, Alice B. "It's a Year 'Round Job." *Library Journal* 78, no. 10 (May 15, 1953): 877–79.

Dana, John Cotton. "Things Every One Should Know." *Bulletin of the Iowa Library Commission* 1, no. 3 (July 1901): 33–35.

Entwisle, Doris R., Karl L. Alexander, and Linda Steffel Olson. *Children, Schools, and Inequality.* Boulder, CO: Westview, 1997.

Fiore, Carole D. *Fiore's Summer Library Reading Program Handbook.* New York: Neal-Schuman, 2005.

Food Research & Action Center. "National School Lunch Program." http://frac.org/ programs/national-school-lunch-program.

———, "Summer Food Mapper." http://frac.org/research/resource-library/summer -food-mapper.

———, "Summer Nutrition Programs." http://frac.org/programs/summer-nutrition -programs.

Goldhor, Herbert, and John McCrossan. "An Exploratory Study of the Effect of a Public Library Summer Reading Club on Reading Skills." *Library Quarterly* 36, no. 1 (January 1966): 14–24.

Haines, Claudia, Cen Campbell, Chip Donohue, and Association for Library Service to Children. *Becoming a Media Mentor: A Guide for Working with Children and Families.* Chicago: American Library Association, 2016.

Harwood Institute. "We Help Individuals and Organizations Turn Outward." www .theharwoodinstitute.org.

Hayes, Clarissa, Randy Rosso, Signe Anderson, and Crystal FitzSimons. "Hunger Doesn't Take a Vacation: Summer Nutrition Status Report." *Food Research & Action Center,* June 2016. http://frac.org/wp-content/uploads/2016_summer _nutrition_report.pdf.

Heyns, Barbara. *Summer Learning and the Effects of Schooling.* New York: Academic, 1978.

Hippel, Paul T. von, Brian Powell, Douglas B. Downey, and Nicholas J. Rowland. "The Effect of School on Overweight in Childhood: Gains in Body Mass Index during the School Year and during Summer Vacation." *American Journal of Public Health* 97, no. 4 (April 2007): 692–704.

Justice, Laura M., Shayne B. Piasta, Janet L. Capps, Stephanie R. Levitt, and Columbus Metropolitan Library. "Library-Based Summer Reading Clubs: Who Participates and Why?" *Library Quarterly: Information, Community, Policy* 83, no. 4 (October 2013): 321–40.

Jyoti, Diana F., Edward A. Frongillo, and Sonya J. Jones. "Food Insecurity Affects School Children's Academic Performance, Weight Gain, and Social Skills." *Journal of Nutrition* 135, no. 12 (December 1, 2005): 2831–39.

Kim, James S., and Thomas G. White. "Scaffolding Voluntary Summer Reading for Children in Grades 3 to 5: An Experimental Study." *Scientific Studies of Reading* 12, no. 1 (2008): 1–23.

Koester, Amy. "Young Children, New Media, & Libraries: Survey Results." Association for Library Service to Children, 2015. www.ala.org/alsc/sites/ala.org.alsc/ files/content/YCNML%20Infographic_0.pdf.

Koester, Amy, Claudia Haines, Dorothy Stoltz, and Cen Campbell. "Media Mentorship in Libraries Serving Youth." Association for Library Service to Children, March 11, 2015. www.ala.org/alsc/sites/ala.org.alsc/files/content/Media%20Mentor ship%20in%20Libraries%20Serving%20Youth_FINAL_no%20graphics.pdf.

Kohn, Alfie. *Punished by Rewards: The Trouble with Gold Stars, Incentive Plans, A's, Praise, and Other Bribes.* Boston: Houghton Mifflin, 1993.

Kotter, John P. *Leading Change.* Boston: Harvard Business School Press, 1996.

Krashen, Stephen D. *The Power of Reading: Insights from the Research.* 2nd ed. Westport, CT: Libraries Unlimited, 2004.

Latimer, Louise P. "Children's Reading Clubs: A Regrettable Movement." *Library Journal* 48, no. 17 (October 1, 1923): 816.

Locke, Jill L. "The Effectiveness of Summer Reading Programs in Public Libraries in the United States." PhD dissertation, School of Library and Information Science, University of Pittsburgh, 1988.

———, "Summer Reading Activities—Way Back When." *Journal of Youth Services in Libraries* 6, no. 1 (Fall 1992): 72–78.

Luby, Joan, Andy Belden, Kelly Botteron, Natasha Marrus, Michael P. Harms, Casey Babb, Tomoyuki Nishino, and Deanna Barch. "The Effects of Poverty on Childhood Brain Development: The Mediating Effect of Caregiving and Stressful Life Events." *JAMA Pediatrics* 167, no. 12 (December 2013): 1135–42.

Matthews, Joe. "Evaluating Summer Reading Programs: Suggested Improvements." *Public Libraries* 49, no. 4 (August 2010): 34–40.

McGill-Franzen, Anne, and Richard L. Allington. "Bridging the Summer Reading Gap." *Instructor* 112, no. 8 (June 2003): 17–19.

McLaughlin, Brenda. "Healthy Summers for Kids: Turning Risk into Opportunity." National Summer Learning Association, May 2012. http://c.ymcdn.com/sites/www.summerlearning.org/resource/resmgr/Healthy_Summers_/NSLA_Healthy_Summers_for_Kid.pdf.

McMillan, Mary Amos. "No Eleventh Book." *Horn Book Magazine* 40, no. 3 (June 1964): 251–54.

Minkel, Walter. "Get with the Program." *School Library Journal* 47, no. 7 (July 2001): 27.

Minneapolis Public Library. "Reading for Credit." *Library Journal* 48, no. 15 (September 1, 1923): 722.

Moore, Anne Carroll. *My Roads to Childhood: Views and Reviews of Children's Books.* Boston: Horn Book, 1961.

Moran, Caitlin. *Moranthology.* New York: Harper Perennial, 2012.

National Academies of Sciences, Engineering, and Medicine. "Summertime Opportunities to Promote Healthy Child and Adolescent Development: Proceedings of a Workshop—in Brief." Washington, DC: National Academies, 2016. doi: 10.17226/24606.

National Summer Learning Association. "Smarter Summers. Brighter Futures." www.summerlearning.org.

No Kid Hungry Center for Best Practices. "Share Our Strength: Summer Meals Survey." March 2013. https://bestpractices.nokidhungry.org/sites/default/files/resources/SOS%20-%20Summer%20Meals%20Survey%20Report%20FINAL2.pdf.

Norton, Michael H., and Emily Dowdall. "Strengthening Networks, Sparking Change: Museums and Libraries as Community Catalysts." *Reinvestment Fund Policy Solutions*, 2016. www.imls.gov/sites/default/files/publications/docments/community-catalyst-report-january-2017.pdf.

Obama, Barack. "Literacy and Education in a 21st-Century Economy." Speech at the Annual Conference of the American Library Association, June 25, 2005. http://obamaspeeches.com/024-Literacy-and-Education-in-a-21st-Century-Economy-Obama-Speech.htm.

Power, Effie L. *Work with Children in Public Libraries*. Chicago: American Library Association, 1943.

Public Library Association. "Project Outcome: Measuring the True Impact of Public Libraries." www.projectoutcome.org.

"Reading Incentive Programs Found to Be 'Highly Commercial.'" *School Library Journal* 41, no. 6 (June 1995): 20.

Reynolds, Kathryn L. "Defending America in the Children's Room: A Summer Reading Plan." *Library Journal* 66, no. 8 (April 15, 1941): 342–44.

Roman, Susan, Deborah T. Carran, and Carole D. Fiore. "The Dominican Study: Public Library Summer Reading Programs Close the Reading Gap." River Forest, IL: Graduate School of Library & Information Science, Dominican University, June 2010. www.oregon.gov/osl/LD/youthsvcs/srp.certificates/dominican study.pdf.

Roman, Susan, and Carole D. Fiore. "Do Public Library Summer Reading Programs Close the Achievement Gap? The Dominican Study." *Children and Libraries* 8, no. 3 (Winter 2010): 27–31.

Rosa, Kathy, ed. "The State of America's Libraries: A Report from the American Library Association: 2015." American Library Association, 2015. www.ala.org/news/sites/ala.org.news/files/content/0415_StateAmLib_0.pdf.

ScholarShare College Savings Plan. "'Read for the Win' Sweepstakes: Official Rules." 2016. www.scholarshare.com/documents/ScholarShare-Summer-Reading -Sweepstakes-Rules-2016.pdf.

Scholastic Inc. "Kids & Family Reading Report." 6th ed. 2017. www.scholastic.com/readingreport/files/Scholastic-KFRR-6ed-2017.pdf.

Scieszka, Jon. *Summer Reading Is Killing Me! The Time Warp Trio 7*. New York: Viking, 1998.

Search Institute. "40 Developmental Assets for Adolescents." www.search-institute .org/content/40-developmental-assets-adolescents-ages-12–18.

Shin, Fay H., and Stephen D. Krashen. *Summer Reading: Program and Evidence*. Boston: Allyn & Bacon, 2008.

Sullivan, Michael. *Fundamentals of Children's Services*. Chicago: American Library Association, 2005.

Summer Matters. "Doesn't Every Child Deserve an Enriching, Memorable Summer?" www.summermatters.net.

———. "Why Summer Matters." www.packard.org/wp-content/uploads/2017/02/Why-Summer-Matters-Infographic.pdf.

United States Department of Agriculture. Food and Nutrition Service. "Capacity Builder." www.fns.usda.gov/capacitybuilder.

———. "Summer Food Service Program." www.fns.usda.gov/sfsp/summer-food-service-program.

Urban Libraries Council. "Accelerate Summer." www.urbanlibraries.org/accelerate-summer-initial-findings-pages-450.php.

———. "Inspiring Libraries. Transforming Communities." www.urbanlibraries.org/about-us-pages-13.php.

———. "Leadership Brief: Libraries Expanding Summer Opportunities." www.urbanlibraries.org/filebin/pdfs/Leadership_Brief_Expanding_Summer.pdf.

Walter, Virginia A. "Summer Reading Research Report." Report submitted to the California Library Association, September 2016.

Walter, Virginia A., and Patricia Garone. "Summer Lunch @ Your Library: Lessons Learned." Report submitted to the California Library Association, December 2016.

Walter, Virginia A., and Penny S. Markey. "Parent Perceptions of a Summer Reading Program." *Journal of Youth Services in Libraries* 11, no. 1 (Fall 1997): 49–65.

Yoke, Beth. "Adopting a Summer Learning Approach for Increased Impact: A YALSA Position Paper." Young Adult Library Services Association, April 22, 2016. www.ala.org/yalsa/adopting-summer-learning-approach-increased-impact-yalsa-position-paper.

Young Adult Library Services Association. *The Complete Summer Reading Program Manual: From Planning to Evaluation.* Chicago: Young Adult Library Services Association, 2012.

Zickuhr, Kathryn, Lee Rainie, Kristen Purcell, and Maeve Duggan. "How Americans Value Public Libraries in Their Communities." Pew Research Center, December 11, 2013. http://libraries.pewinternet.org/files/legacy-pdf/PIP_Libraries%20in%20communities.pdf.

ABOUT THE AUTHORS

Natalie Cole is a library programs consultant at the California State Library. Previously, she was interim executive director at the California Library Association where she also led the California Summer Reading Program and the Lunch at the Library program. She received her MA and PhD in Librarianship from the University of Sheffield, UK.

Virginia A. Walter has the MLS degree from the University of California, Berkeley, and a PhD in Public Administration from the University of Southern California. She has more than 20 years experience working in California public libraries, followed by 20 years as a tenured faculty member in the Information Studies Department at UCLA. She is currently an Emerita Professor, retaining an office on campus with continuing responsibilities for advising students and teaching one class per year. In addition to her teaching experience at UCLA, she taught classes in Young Adult Services at the University of Zadar as a Fulbright Scholar.

INDEX